AN ANTHOLOGY OF
OLD ENGLISH POETRY

AN ANTHOLOGY OF

Old English Poetry

Translated into Alliterative Verse by

CHARLES W. KENNEDY, 1882 –

*Murray Professor of English Literature, Emeritus
Princeton University*

NEW YORK

OXFORD UNIVERSITY PRESS

1960

© 1960 by Oxford University Press, Inc.

Library of Congress Catalogue Card Number: 59–11753

Sixth Printing, 1968

Printed in the United States of America

PREFACE

THIS Anthology is intended for readers who may wish to explore the riches of Old English poetry but find themselves shut out by the barrier of language. It has been my purpose to present in translation selections from Old English verse so chosen as to illustrate its variety of type, its scope of subject matter, and its poetic excellence. The task has been a pleasant one. We of the English tongue are fortunate heirs of a rich poetic heritage extending deep into European backgrounds, and written in England during the period from the seventh century to the end of the tenth.

From this body of poetry, it has been my endeavor to translate selections into a modern verse faithful to the Old English text and, as far as linguistic changes permit, suggestive of the alliterative rhythms of the Anglo-Saxon originals. In so sensitive a task success is not easy. The translator in the end can only hope that from this distant past these translations may catch some gleam of sunlight from an ancient world.

Of my translations in this volume some are old, some are new. My *Old English Elegies* and *The Earliest English Poetry* have for some time been out of print. I am happy to have this opportunity to republish the translations of the *Elegies*, as well as certain selections from *The Earliest English Poetry*. *The Battle of Maldon* I have newly translated and much of the poetry in the chapters dealing with the *Gnomic Verse* and the poems of Continental tradition. No Anthology could be adequate without illustration of the nature and quality of the longer poems such as *Beowulf*, the *Phoenix*, the Fall of Man from *Genesis*, and the Last Judgment of *Christ 3*. For permission to reprint selections from my translations of these poems in *Beowulf* and *Early English Christian Poetry*, I offer my sincere thanks to Oxford University Press.

Finally, for me there are interwoven with the lines of these poems long memories of pleasant association with graduate students at Princeton who were studying the language and literature of Anglo-Saxon England. They were both students and friends, and their friendship enriched the years.

C. W. K.

March 25, 1959
Princeton, N. J.

CONTENTS

INTRODUCTION

OLD ENGLISH POETRY, the Anglo-Saxon vernacular verse composed in England before the Norman Conquest, constitutes one of the richest medieval traditions in any modern European tongue. The period extending from the middle of the seventh century to the end of the tenth has left us a body of verse outstanding in variety and literary excellence. It was the product partly of an ancient culture which had come to England with the Germanic Settlement of the fifth and early sixth centuries, and partly of the transforming influences of the age in which it was written, an age of change and growth during which Germanic strains were slowly moulded by the influence of medieval learning and the Latin culture of the Christian Church.

The successive waves of the Settlement had brought to England a store of Continental tradition: myth and saga, folk-tale and chronicle, legends long known among the Germanic tribes, and now remembered and retold in England. A race does not easily lose memory of its past, even in the dark centuries and upon foreign soil. Tradition may grow obscure with passing years, and alien strains engraft themselves on ancient legend in strange and puzzling ways. But tradition persists, and the past lives on. In the songs of the early English, and in the lays that enlivened their banquets, old memories lingered, famous names and

heroic deeds of chronicle and legend. The singer was an English minstrel, but often the song re-echoed a Continental past. Through the
dusk of their great halls resounded the glory of heroes long dead: Attila
the Hun and Eormanric the Goth, Theodoric and his thanes, Hildeburh
of Finnsburg, Sigemund and Signy of the Volsungs, Walther of Aquitaine and his lady Hildegund, Beowulf of the Geats, shapes of the dead
stirring to resurrection as the gleeman sang.

In this body of tradition came also the secret learning of the wise men
and the folk-wisdom of the people: runic letters of mysterious meaning
and power, magic charms against ill-fortune and disease, a folk-lore of
herbs and simples, and the homely wisdoms of experience set forth in
proverbs and gnomic verse. The Germanic Settlers carved their crude
runic inscriptions on English stone, and on the utensils and weapons
of early English life. In rude verse they chanted their pagan charms to
defend their fields from barrenness, and their bodies from the aches and
pains of rheumatic winters. In time of danger and doubt they appealed
to the gnomic wisdom of their forefathers.

From of old the Settlers were at home on the sea, ranging widely in
all weathers in their long, dragon-prowed Viking ships. As is true of all
experienced mariners, their love of the salt sea-streams was tempered by
a wholesome respect for the destructive might of ocean. *The Seafarer,*
one of the most memorable of the elegies, celebrates at length, and with
alternating stress, this bittersweet blending of attraction and fear. Old
English poetry is filled with superb descriptive passages dealing with
ocean-voyaging by night and day, in fair weather and foul.

The world of nature that hedged men about was stubborn and harsh.

The years were reckoned by the passing of the winters. Darkness and cold, the freezing hardships of winter on land and sea, the haunting fear of danger lurking in the shadows after the sun was gone, these are themes that set the grim mood for much of the early verse. But the long severity of their winter months brought by contrast a joy in returning Spring, "the sunny and shining days that ever observe their season," the time of "greening meadows and blossoming earth, and the music of bird-calls." Not a few passages of Old English verse contain brief, vivid realisms of Spring mood which make them memorable.

Much in the world of nature was of course unknown and terrifying. Superstitious imagination peopled the dark with warlocks and witches, gnomes and trolls, a malign and haunting crew of evil spirits. In their malevolent and capricious interference in the lives of men was to be found, it seemed, the secret source of misfortune such as sickness or loss of property, and of sudden tragic disaster for which no immediate cause seemed obvious. From this same mysterious nature were culled the means to combat such evils. Folk-knowledge of herbs and simples was blended with superstition in the fashioning of magic herbal decoctions used with rituals and formulas of transfer and exorcism. As time passed, these pagan charms were altered by the gradual influence of the Christian faith, and the sutures joining the ancient pagan and later Christian elements are often easily discernible. The *Charm for Unfruitful Land* is a case in point.

The Settlement brought with it simple codes of conduct and grim ways of life. Worship of the Germanic gods was a rude and savage cult. The ancient myths symbolized a titanic warfare between the kindlier forces of nature and those hostile powers by whose ruthless strength man's life and even the might of the gods themselves were menaced. Fate brooded over all, a dark inexorable power shrouded behind numbing hardship and mortal danger. To the living of life the strong man brought heroic courage and stoic endurance. Fate would sometimes spare, if valor held out.

The *Germania* of Tacitus provides a vivid estimate of the characteristics of early Germanic tribal life, out of which grew many of the qualities which entered into the Settlement of England. The stress on courage and the love of battle, reflected in so many passages of Old English verse, seem from the beginning to have been rooted in the Germanic strain. Personal loyalty and group loyalty were central in the moral code of the Settlers: loyalty to friend, to leader, and to clan. Loyalty to leader must be absolute. The spirit of the Germanic *comitatus*, with its reciprocal obligations of protection and reward on the one side, and loyalty and service on the other, colors the material of many a passage in Old English verse, and survives undiminished as late as *Maldon*. A retainer who had lost his lord was of all men most wretched, a lonely exile who could find no solace for his loss, no substitute for the tie that had been broken. The lament of *The Wanderer* is the classic passage for illustration of so tragic a grief.

The corpus of Old English verse gives evidence of the extent to which Englishmen of the seventh and eighth centuries still preserved race memories rooted in Germanic tradition, and enriched their poetry by borrowings from Continental legend and annals. Such poems as *Widsith*, *Deor's Lament*, and the *Waldere* and *Finnsburg* fragments, give testimony to this debt, as does the *Beowulf* in its tale of Sigemund, its lay of Finn, and its reflection of Scandinavian and Icelandic analogues.

With the conversion of England to the Christian faith there came a refinement of the scale of human values, a sensitizing of men's minds and moods, which swelled the currents of life, and varied and colored the play of poetic invention. To the early epic tales and songs of battle were added versifications of Biblical and Apocryphal themes, of lives of the saints, of martyrologies. The poetic mood turned from earlier forms to hymns of adoration, dream-visions, and prophetic verse. In this expansion, the reader is aware of the shaping energy of Christian learning: of the moulding force of Biblical exegesis and the Catholic liturgy, of Hexaemeral and Apocalyptic tradition, of ecclesiastical dogma and doctrine.

The religious poetry reflects both Classical and Christian culture. It is not to be forgotten that the poetry of the eighth and ninth centuries was written at a time when men of learning were familiar with the works of Aristotle and Cicero, or that Old English poetry contains elements that show the influence of Lucretius, Pliny, and Virgil. Alcuin's list of authors available in the Library at York includes their names, and Lucretius is cited and a line from the Sixth Book of Lucretius is quoted by Isidore of Seville, whose writings influenced the *De Natura Rerum* of Bede.

Most of all, these religious poems reveal their debt to the writings of medieval scholars: to Alcuin and Augustine, to Gregory and Bede, to Boethius and Lactantius, and to many others. In the fabric of this religious verse, moreover, threads of the earlier secular verse were blended.

Conventional elements of landscape and seascape, characteristic details of weather, a stereotyped imagery of loyalty and warfare, these are found as decorative elements in the religious poems.

Generally speaking, the authorship of this body of Old English verse, secular and religious, is almost unknown. Except for the Caedmon tradition as related by Bede, and the rune signatures of Cynewulf in *Juliana, Elene, Christ 2,* and the *Fates of the Apostles,* Old English poetry is of uncertain authorship and somewhat uncertain date. Caedmon's *Hymn* can be assigned to a date not far from 670. The spelling of Cynewulf's name in his runic signatures suggests the period from 750 to 800 for his signed poems. *Genesis B,* a dramatically vivid interpolation in the text of *Genesis,* is probably later than the middle of the ninth century, if its Old Saxon original is correctly dated as about 830 or 840. The battle poems of *Brunanburh* and *Maldon* were presumably written not long after the battles they commemorate, that is, 937, and 991.

Old English poetry was composed in a flexible type of four-stress, alliterative line consisting of two half-lines of two stresses each, separated by a strongly marked caesural pause. The stressed syllables established the rhythm, and the two half-lines were bound into a unit by the convention of alliteration. Variation in the relative positions of stresses within the line, and a convention of subordinate stresses, produced delicate and subtle currents of mutation and change of rhythm. The recitation of this alliterative verse was usually accompanied by chords struck on the harp.

The occurrence of rhyme is infrequent. Cynewulf uses it in a passage of fifteen lines near the end of the *Elene,* and a more extended passage is found in the eighty-seven lines of the *Rhyme Poem* of the Exeter Book. In a few other poems rhyme occurs in brief passages. Its occasional use may perhaps be traced to an influence of rhyming Latin hymns familiar to religious poets.

Estimated as a whole, Old English poetry expresses in many ways the changing spirit of the age. It was a period during which the limited perspectives of a pagan world were being gradually widened by the Christian philosophy. The stark and primitive social codes expressive of Germanic folkways were being transformed by the spiritual demands of Christian ethics. The Old English world was beginning to find room for a new frame of reference for the thoughts and strivings of men.

It will always remain true, I think, for many readers who love this ancient verse, that it stands as a testimonial, even if an imperfect one, of a way of life reborn and reshaped by the life-giving touch of the Christian faith, and the ecclesiastical culture of the medieval Church. As these influences enfranchised the thoughts and moulded the lives of men, their poetry, too, was transformed. The dark legends and narrow folkways of the pagan past died into silence, and poets sang with joy of a new way of life, and of the shining symbols which have served to shape the nature and destiny of the Christian world.

One of the dominant characteristics of the religious poetry is its fusion of sensitive religious faith with the shaping and vitalizing imagination and emotion of the poet. If the life of Cynewulf, for example, was in any way a cloistered one, his poetry is marked by no aloofness from the world. He was a lover of the human scene with a sense of its fugitive loveliness. He had a kindly understanding of the human heart.

In this body of Old English poetry much is excellent; a part is timeless. In it the old Germanic recognition of life's flinty necessities is still implicit, and strength-giving; as is also the conviction of man's imperative need of loyalty and courage. But the centuries of the English conversion had brought wider vision and longer thoughts. The heartbreak of the elegies, the fortitude of the battle poems, the antique grace and energy of the religious allegories, the gentle and lonely accents of Cynewulf, the lyric adoration of *A Dream of the Rood*, such poetry is memorable in any age. Finest of all is the *Beowulf*. In it, as in the poems of Cynewulf and his school, we find the most adequate poetic symbols of an age which touched life with the light of wider horizons, and shaped new hopes for the hearts of men.

I

ELEGIES AND DRAMATIC LYRICS

ELEGIES AND DRAMATIC LYRICS

The clear lyric strain which has poured its melody and passion into English verse through the centuries has early illustration in four Old English poems from the Exeter Book. Two of these lyrics, *The Wanderer* and *The Ruin*, are elegiac in mood. Two others, *The Wife's Lament* and *The Husband's Message*, are love poems or dramatic lyrics.

The two elegies differ markedly in mood and pattern from the personal elegy. Their range of interest is universal, deriving from a moving sense of the tragedy of life itself — a consciousness of the transience of earthly joy, and the inexorable limitation of man's existence by the mutable and mortal.

The Wanderer is the lament of a man who has lost his lord. Loosed from primitive loyalties to clan or leader, and lacking favor or protection, he has become in a very special sense a man adrift. Nowhere in Old English poetry has the misery attending this forlorn fate received more vivid, detailed, and emotional presentment.

The Ruin is an elegiac fragment setting forth the poet's musings on the ruins of a fortress, or city. Broken walls and towers, and shattered roofs of tile, now mark a site where once stood splendid banqueting halls and Roman baths. The reference to hot baths has led to a suggestion that the poem is describing Roman ruins of the city of Bath.

The Wife's Lament and *The Husband's Message* are in one sense companion poems, in another sense poems in contrast. The central theme of each poem is the separation of husband and wife. In *The Wife's Lament* her husband has crossed the sea, and in his absence his kinsmen, plotting a permanent separation of husband and wife, have condemned her to a dwelling in a solitary cave under an oak tree. Here she gives expression to her wretchedness and continuing love.

3

In *The Husband's Message* the husband has been forced by a vendetta to flee from his native land to a country beyond the sea. Now he sends back a "message staff" asking his wife to join him. The speaker is the staff itself telling how once it grew as a sapling near the sea. Now knife's point and man's skill have carved it with runic letters to bring a message only the wife can understand. The husband reminds her of the pledges they plighted of old. Now he has wealth and a lordly estate in a new land. One thing only he lacks — reunion with the "prince's daughter" to whom he is pledged. Let her take ship and sail to join him. At this point the five runic letters of the text assume at least a shadowy meaning. They may be the initial letters of five names, known to the wife, who stand as "oath-helpers," or guarantors of the husband's good faith, in this reaffirmation of his former vows.

The Wanderer

Oft to the Wanderer,   weary of exile,
Cometh God's pity,   compassionate love,
Though woefully toiling   on wintry seas
With churning oar   in the icy wave,
Homeless and helpless   he fled from Fate.
Thus saith the Wanderer   mindful of misery,
Grievous disasters,   and death of kin:

   "Oft when the day broke,   oft at the dawning,
Lonely and wretched   I wailed my woe.
No man is living,   no comrade left,
To whom I dare fully   unlock my heart.
I have learned truly   the mark of a man
Is keeping his counsel   and locking his lips,
Let him think what he will !   For, woe of heart
Withstandeth not Fate;   a failing spirit
Earneth no help.   Men eager for honor
Bury their sorrow   deep in the breast.

   "So have I also,   often in wretchedness
Fettered my feelings,   far from my kin,
Homeless and hapless,   since days of old,
When the dark earth   covered my dear lord's face,
And I sailed away   with sorrowful heart,
Over wintry seas,   seeking a gold-lord,
If far or near   lived one to befriend me
With gift in the mead-hall   and comfort for grief.

   "Who bears it, knows   what a bitter companion,
Shoulder to shoulder,   sorrow can be,
When friends are no more.   His fortune is exile,
Not gifts of fine gold;   a heart that is frozen,
Earth's winsomeness dead.   And he dreams of the hall-men,
The dealing of treasure,   the days of his youth,
When his lord bade welcome   to wassail and feast.

But gone is that gladness,   and never again
Shall come the loved counsel   of comrade and king.
    "Even in slumber   his sorrow assaileth,
And, dreaming he claspeth   his dear lord again,
Head on knee, hand on knee,   loyally laying,
Pledging his liege   as in days long past.
Then from his slumber   he starts lonely-hearted,
Beholding gray stretches   of tossing sea,
Sea-birds bathing,   with wings outspread,
While hailstorms darken,   and driving snow.
Bitterer then   is the bane of his wretchedness,
The longing for loved one: his grief is renewed.
The forms of his kinsmen   take shape in the silence;
In rapture he greets them;   in gladness he scans
Old comrades remembered.   But they melt into air
With no word of greeting   to gladden his heart.
Then again surges   his sorrow upon him;
And grimly he spurs   his weary soul
Once more to the toil   of the tossing sea.
    "No wonder therefore,   in all the world,
If a shadow darkens   upon my spirit
When I reflect   on the fates of men—
How one by one   proud warriors vanish
From the halls that knew them,   and day by day
All this earth ages   and droops unto death.
No man may know wisdom   till many a winter
Has been his portion.   A wise man is patient,
Not swift to anger,   nor hasty of speech,
Neither too weak,   nor too reckless, in war,
Neither fearful nor fain,   nor too wishful of wealth,
Nor too eager in vow—   ere he know the event.
A brave man must bide   when he speaketh his boast
Until he know surely   the goal of his spirit.
    "A wise man will ponder   how dread is that doom
When all this world's wealth   shall be scattered and waste

As now, over all,   through the regions of earth,
Walls stand rime-covered   and swept by the winds.
The battlements crumble,   the wine-halls decay;
Joyless and silent   the heroes are sleeping
Where the proud host fell   by the wall they defended.
Some battle launched   on their long, last journey;
One a bird bore   o'er the billowing sea;
One the gray wolf slew;   one a grieving eorl
Sadly gave   to the grave's embrace.
The Warden of men   hath wasted this world
Till the sound of music   and revel is stilled,
And these giant-built structures   stand empty of life.
   "He who shall muse   on these mouldering ruins,
And deeply ponder   this darkling life,
Must brood on old legends   of battle and bloodshed,
And heavy the mood   that troubles his heart:
'Where now is the warrior?   Where is the war horse?
Bestowal of treasure,   and sharing of feast?
Alas! the bright ale-cup,   the byrny-clad warrior,
The prince in his splendor   —those days are long sped
In the night of the past,   as if they never had been !'
And now remains only,   for warriors' memorial,
A wall wondrous high   with serpent shapes carved.
Storms of ash-spears   have smitten the eorls,
Carnage of weapon,   and conquering Fate.
   "Storms now batter   these ramparts of stone;
Blowing snow   and the blast of winter
Enfold the earth;   night-shadows fall
Darkly lowering,   from the north driving
Raging hail   in wrath upon men.
Wretchedness fills   the realm of earth,
And Fate's decrees   transform the world.
Here wealth is fleeting,   friends are fleeting,
Man is fleeting,   maid is fleeting;
All the foundation of earth   shall fail!"

Thus spake the sage   in solitude pondering.
Good man is he   who guardeth his faith.
He must never too quickly   unburden his breast
Of its sorrow, but eagerly   strive for redress;
And happy the man   who seeketh for mercy
From his heavenly Father,   our Fortress and Strength.

The Ruin

Wondrous this masonry   wasted by Fate!
Giant-built battlements   shattered and broken!
The roofs are in ruin,   the towers are wrecked,
The frost-covered bastions   battered and fallen.
Rime whitens mortar;   the cracking walls
Have sagged and toppled,   weakened by Time.
The clasp of earth   and the clutch of the grave
Grip the proud builders,   long perished and gone,
While a hundred generations   have run.
Hoary with lichen   and ruddy of hue
This wall has outlasted,   unshaken by storm,
Reign after reign;   now ravaged and wrecked
The lofty arch   is leveled in ruin. . . .
   Firmly the builder   laid the foundations,
Cunningly bound them   with iron bands;
Stately the palaces,   splendid the baths,
Towers and pinnacles   pointing on high;
Many a mead-hall   rang with their revelry,
Many a court   with the clangor of arms,
Till Fate the all-leveling   laid them low.
A pestilence rose   and corpses were rife,
And death laid hold   on the warrior-host.
   Then their bulwarks were broken,   their fortresses fell,
The hands to restore them   were helpless and still.
Desolate now are the courts,   and the dome,

8

With arches discolored,   is stripped of its tiles.
Where of old once the warrior   walked in his pride,
Gleaming with gold   and wanton with wine,
Splendidly shining   in glittering mail,
The structure lies fallen   and scattered in ruin.
Around him he saw   a treasure of silver,
Riches of pearl   and precious stones,
In a shining city   of far-flung sway.
There stood courts of stone,   with a gushing spring
Of boiling water   in welling floods,
And a wall embosomed   in gleaming embrace
The spot where the hot baths   burst into air.

The Wife's Lament

A song I sing   of sorrow unceasing,
The tale of my trouble,   the weight of my woe,
Woe of the present,   and woe of the past,
Woe never-ending   of exile and grief,
But never since girlhood   greater than now.
First, the pang   when my lord departed,
Far from his people,   beyond the sea;
Bitter the heartache   at break of dawn,
The longing for rumor   in what far land
So weary a time   my loved one tarried.
Far I wandered then,   friendless and homeless,
Seeking for help   in my heavy need.
   With secret plotting   his kinsmen purposed
To wedge us apart,   wide worlds between,
And bitter hate.   I was sick at heart.
Harshly my lord   bade lodge me here.
In all this land   I had few to love me,
Few that were loyal,   few that were friends.
Wherefore my spirit   is heavy with sorrow
To learn my beloved,   my dear man and mate
Bowed by ill-fortune   and bitter in heart,
Is masking his purpose   and planning a wrong.
With blithe hearts   often of old we boasted
That nought should part us   save death alone;
All that has failed   and our former love
Is now as if   it had never been!
Far or near   where I fly there follows
The hate of him   who was once so dear.
   In this forest-grove   they have fixed my abode
Under an oak   in a cavern of earth,
An old cave-dwelling   of ancient days,
Where my heart is crushed   by the weight of my woe.
Gloomy its depths   and the cliffs that o'erhang it,
Grim are its confines   with thorns overgrown—

A joyless dwelling   where daily the longing
For an absent loved one   brings anguish of heart.
    Lovers there are   who may live their love,
Joyously keeping   the couch of bliss,
While I in my earth-cave   under the oak
Pace to and fro   in the lonely dawn.
Here must I sit   through the summer-long day,
Here must I weep   in affliction and woe;
Yet never, indeed,   shall my heart know rest
From all its anguish,   and all its ache,
Wherewith life's burdens   have brought me low.
    Ever man's years   are subject to sorrow,
His heart's thoughts bitter,   though his bearing be blithe;
Troubled his spirit,   beset with distress—
Whether all wealth   of the world be his lot,
Or hunted by Fate   in a far country
My beloved is sitting   soul-weary and sad,
Swept by the storm,   and stiff with the frost,
In a wretched cell   under rocky cliffs
By severing waters   encircled about—
Sharpest of sorrows   my lover must suffer
Remembering always   a happier home.
Woeful his fate   whose doom is to wait
With longing heart   for an absent love.

The Husband's Message

In the sand I grew,   by the rocky sea-wall
Near the surf firm-rooted   in fixed abode.
Few were the men   who beheld my refuge
In the lonely reaches   beside the sea;
Only the dark wave   at the day's dawning
Sportively bound me   in flowing embrace.
Little I weened   that I, who was voiceless,
Should ever hold speech,   or discourse at the feast.
That is a marvel   amazing the mind
Of those who know little   of such-like things
How a knife's sharp edge,   and a strong hand's skill,
Steel's keen point,   and man's cunning craft,
Purposely planned me,   assigned me my part
To give thee a message   that we two may grasp,
To utter it boldly,   yet so that no other
May publish abroad   the words I report.

   To thine ear only   I tell the tale
How first as a sapling   I flourished and grew. . . .
In the hold of a ship,   o'er the salt sea-streams,
Where my liege lord sent me   oft I have sailed.
Now in a bark's bosom   here am I borne.
Now shalt thou learn   of my lord's loyal love;
His enduring affection   I dare to affirm.

   Lady ring-laden,   he bade me implore thee,
Who carved this wood,   that thou call to mind
The pledges you plighted   before you were parted,
While still in the same land   together you shared
A lordly home   and the rapture of love,
Before a feud   drove him far from his folk.
He it is bids me   eagerly urge
When from the hill slope,   out of the wood,
Thou hearest the cuckoo   plaintively calling,
Haste thee to ship   on the tossing sea.
Let no living man, then,   delay thee in sailing,

Stay thee in leaving   or stop thee in flight.
    Spread thy sail   on the home of the sea-mew,
Take seat in thy galley,   and steer away south
To where o'er the sea-lane   thy lover awaits.
No greater bliss   could his heart engage
In all the world   —'twas his word to me—
If God the Almighty   would grant you two
To dwell together   and deal out gifts,
To tried retainers,   of treasure and rings.
He hath abundance   of beaten gold. . . .
Now in a far land   my lord holds in fee
Home and fair fields   though here once of old,
Fated and lonely,   need forced him to flight,
Launching his ship   on the lanes of the deep,
Churning the sea-streams   in haste to escape.
    Now his troubles are over   and all distress,
He lacks no wealth   that the heart may wish,
Jewels and horses   and joys of the hall,
Nor any fair treasure   that earth can afford.
O Prince's daughter!   if he may possess thee,
To add to the pledges   ye plighted of old,
Here S and R   together I set,
EA, W, and D,   by oath to declare
That while life lasts   so long he'll be faithful
To lover's vow   and to true love's pledge
Which often ye plighted   in days of old.

II

SEA POETRY

SEA POETRY

English poetry from the beginning has had as a favorite theme the influence in men's lives of the varying moods and might of the sea. From the Old English period it has reflected the actualities of ocean life with such faithful directness that the poetic rendering is as expressive of the nineteenth century as of the ninth.

This strain in Old English verse is well illustrated by portions of six poems which include the theme of ocean-voyaging: *The Seafarer* of the Exeter Book; *Noah's Flood* from *Genesis*; *The Parting of the Red Sea* from *Exodus*; *Helena Embarks for Palestine* from Cynewulf's *Elene*; *The Voyage of Life* from Cynewulf's *Christ 2*; and *St. Andrew's Voyage to Mermedonia* from *Andreas*.

In *The Seafarer* the hardship, loneliness, and danger of wintry voyages in uncharted seas, and the lure and fascination that intertwine even with knowledge of peril, these attributes of the sailor's life are set forth with sensitive faithfulness. *Noah's Flood* follows the simplicity of Biblical narrative. But there is poetic vividness in the description of the rains that caused the Flood, and a touch of Old English realism in the birds that Noah sends out from the ark. The raven is depicted as the Old English battle-scavenger. The foul one "perched on the floating corpses. The dusky-feathered would not return." The dove, in its three flights to scan the receding waters, is drawn with warm touches that suggest the intimacy of St. Guthlac and the birds. Similarly, in *The Parting of the Red Sea* a naïvely realistic visualization of uncovered ocean-bottoms, whereon man's foot had never been set before, makes the passage memorable.

Helena Embarks for Palestine, brief as it is, is one of the most finished of these sea-voyages, combining a detailed embarkation scene with the voyage itself, and ending with the debarkation and march inland. *The Voyage of Life* is an illustration of Cynewulf's poetic skill in expanding Gregory's brief suggestion about "fixing the anchor of hope upon an eternal fatherland" into an artistically complete and detailed ocean simile.

The most sustained account of an ocean voyage in Old English poetry is the voyage of St. Andrew to Mermedonia. Andrew's voyage, undertaken at God's command, is in a ship of which God Himself is Shipman and two angels the sailors, although throughout the voyage they remain unknown. With these elements of miracle are combined some of the finest realisms in Old English sea poetry. The sailing at daybreak (235-351), the storm at sea (369-381), and Andrew's expression of his admiration of the Shipman's seamanship (471-520), are superbly done.

The Seafarer *

A song I sing   of my sea-adventure,
The strain of peril,   the stress of toil,
Which oft I endured   in anguish of spirit
Through weary hours   of aching woe.
My bark was swept   by the breaking seas;
Bitter the watch   from the bow by night
As my ship drove on   within sound of the rocks.
My feet were numb   with the nipping cold,
Hunger sapped   a sea-weary spirit,
And care weighed heavy   upon my heart.
   Little the landlubber,   safe on shore,
Knows what I've suffered   in icy seas
Wretched and worn   by the winter storms,
Hung with icicles,   stung by hail,
Lonely and friendless   and far from home.
In my ears no sound   but the roar of the sea,
The icy combers,   the cry of the swan;
In place of the mead-hall   and laughter of men
My only singing   the sea-mew's call,
The scream of the gannet,   the shriek of the gull;
Through the wail of the wild gale   beating the bluffs
The piercing cry   of the ice-coated petrel,
The storm-drenched eagle's echoing scream.
In all my wretchedness,   weary and lone,
I had no comfort   of comrade or kin.
   Little indeed can he credit,   whose town-life
Pleasantly passes   in feasting and joy,
Sheltered from peril,   what weary pain
Often I've suffered   in foreign seas.
Night shades darkened   with driving snow
From the freezing north,   and the bonds of frost
Firm-locked the land,   while falling hail,

* The Seafarer 1–64.

Coldest of kernels,   encrusted earth.
    Yet still, even now,   my spirit within me
Drives me seaward   to sail the deep,
To ride the long swell   of the salt sea-wave.
Never a day   but my heart's desire
Would launch me forth   on the long sea-path,
Fain of far harbors   and foreign shores.
Yet lives no man   so lordly of mood,
So eager in giving,   so ardent in youth,
So bold in his deeds,   or so dear to his lord,
Who is free from dread   in his far sea-travel,
Or fear of God's purpose   and plan for his fate.
The beat of the harp,   and bestowal of treasure,
The love of woman,   and worldly hope,
Nor other interest   can hold his heart
Save only the sweep   of the surging billows;
His heart is haunted   by love of the sea.
    Trees are budding   and towns are fair,
Meadows kindle   and all life quickens,
All things hasten   the eager-hearted,
Who joyeth therein,   to journey afar,
Turning seaward   to distant shores.
The cuckoo stirs him   with plaintive call,
The herald of summer,   with mournful song,
Foretelling the sorrow   that stabs the heart.
Who liveth in luxury,   little he knows
What woe men endure   in exile's doom.
    Yet still, even now,   my desire outreaches,
My spirit soars   over tracts of sea,
O'er the home of the whale,   and the world's expanse.
Eager, desirous,   the lone sprite returneth;
It cries in my ears   and it urges my heart
To the path of the whale   and the plunging sea.

Noah's Flood *

Then the Lord God spoke   and said unto Noah:
"With a great flood   I will destroy this folk
And every kind   of living creature
That fill the sky   and swim the sea,
Birds of air,   and beasts of the field.
But thou shalt be saved,   and thy sons also,
When the dark waters,   the destroying deep,
Shall swallow the hosts   of sinful men.

"Begin to build thee a ship,   a mighty wave-house;
Make room for many   and a rightful place
For every creature,   each after its kind.
Build floors   in the ark's bosom;
Fashion it well   fifty ells wide,
Thirty ells high,   three hundred ells long,
And fasten it firm   against the flood.
Within it lead offspring   of all that live,
Seed of all flesh,   and the ark shall hold them.". . .

After many winters   All-Wielding God
Saw the greatest of sea-houses   towering high,
Noah's vessel well fastened   within and without,
And preserved with pitch   against the flood.
It was best of all ships,   a special kind
Growing more safe   as the breaking seas
And black sea-streams   beat up against it. . . .

And Noah embarked   boarding the wave-ship
As God gave bidding,   leading his sons
And their wives with them; and all God willed
To preserve for seed   went into the ark
As the Almighty   had given command.
There behind them   the Warden of heaven,
The Lord of victory,   locked the door
Of the ocean-house   with His own hands,

* *Genesis* 1294–1313; 1320–26; 1356–99; 1441–82.

And with His blessing   the Lord God blessed
All in the ark.   Now the son of Lamech,
Old and wise,   had six hundred winters
When he boarded the ark   with dear ones and sons.
    Then the Lord unloosed   the rain from the heavens,
Let roaring torrents   and rushing streams
From every channel   overflow the world.
Over the shore's barrier   the sea surged up;
Strong was He and stern   Who ruled the waters!
The dark flood covered   the children of evil,
Laid waste their realm   and their native land.
God visited their sins   on the sons of men!
For forty days   and forty nights
The sea laid hold   on that fated folk.
Fierce the affliction   and deadly to men;
The stormy surges   of the King of glory
Snatched life from body   of those sinful men.
The raging flood,   heaving beneath the heavens
Covered high hills   throughout the wide world,
On its bosom uplifted   the ark from the earth
And all living things   which the Lord had blessed
When He locked behind them   the door of the ship.
Then over the deep,   under the heavens,
That best of dwellings   and the burden it bore
Were driven afar.   No watery terror
Could touch those sailors   for Holy God
Saved them and ferried them.   Fifteen ells deep
Over the hills   lay the heaving flood.
'Twas a fearful fate! . . .
    Then after long days   the son of Lamech
From the ark let fly   a black-feathered raven
Over the steep flood.   Noah counted it sure,
If in its flight   it could find no land,
The raven would return   unto the ark
Over the wide waters.   But Noah's hope failed!
The foul one perched   on the floating corpses;
The dusky-feathered   would not return.

Then seven days   after the dark raven,
He let a gray dove   over the deep
Fly from the ark   to try if the flood
Had ebbed from the ground   of the green earth.
Widely she sought her desire   circling afar
But nowhere found rest.   Because of the flood
She could find no land   with her feet,
Nor light on a leaf   of any tree
Because of the sea-streams.   The steep hills
Were covered with water.   The wild bird
Flew back at evening   over the dusky waves
Unto the ark   settling weary,
And hungry, into the hand   of that holy man.
    And again after seven days   a second wild dove
Was sent from the ark.   She flew afar,
Exulting in flight,   till she found a perch
And resting place in a tree.   She was happy-hearted
That weary of wing   she could sit on the shining boughs.
She shook her feathers   and flew back with her gift,
To Noah's hand bringing   a twig of an olive tree,
With leaves growing green. The lord of the shipmen knew
That comfort at last was come,   requital for danger and toil.
    And after a third week   Noah sent out a dove;
But she flew not back to the ark.   She found dry land,
And came to green forests.   Never again
Would she rest glad-hearted   under the ark's dark roof.
Nor was there need!

The Parting of the Red Sea *

The band of the bold   were gathered together,
Ready to advance;   their banner rode high,
Brightest of beacons.   And all abode
Nigh to the sea   till their gleaming guide
Broke the cloud barrier,   shining on shield.
   Then before the host   a herald stood forth,
A valiant leader   uplifting his shield,
Commanding the captains   to silence their troops
That many might hear   their lord's behest.
The people's shepherd   fain would speak
With holy voice   before the host;
In words of worth   their leader addressed them:
"Fear not though Pharaoh   may bring against us
An army of sword-men,   a legion of eorls.
This day our God   shall give them reward!
They shall not live longer   to vex us with woe;
Have no fear of the doomed,   or the fated for death.
Their fleeting race   has run to its end. . . .
   "Watch, dear people;   behold a wonder:
With right hand grasping   this green rod
I smote the sea. The waves rise up,
The waters form   a rampart wall.
The sea is thrust aside!   The sands are dry,
Gray army-roads,   ancient foundations
(Whereon I never   in all the world
Heard said that man   set foot before),
Shining plains,   imprisoned deep-sea bottoms
Which from of old the waters   covered with waves.
The South Wind,   breath of the ocean,
Has blown them back.   The deep is divided.
The ebb tide spewed up sand.   And well I know
God, the Almighty,   has granted you grace,

_____
* *Exodus* 247–68; 278–306.

24

You bronze-clad eorls! Now haste is best
That you may be free from clutch of the foe,
Since God has raised these Red Sea streams
Into a rampart. The walls of water are reared
To the roof of clouds, a wondrous road in the sea."
    After these words the warriors rose,
The band of the valiant. The sea lay still.
On the sand the legion uplifted their banners,
Their bright linden bucklers. For Israel's host
The wall of water stood upright all the long day;
The resolute eorls were shielded with sure defense.

Helena Embarks for Palestine *

Then Constantine, mindful   of the Holy Cross,
Bade his mother fare   over the floodway
To search with many   where the Tree of splendor,
The Holy Rood,   was hid in earth,
The Cross of heaven's King.   Nor was Helena slow
In sailing, nor slighted   the word of her son,
Her giver of good.   Soon was she ready
For the pleasing voyage   as the prince of men,
Of mail-clad warriors,   gave her command.

   A host of eorls   made haste to the shore;
Sea-horses stood ready   at the ocean's rim,
Bridled sea-stallions   breasting the waves.
The lady's departure   was plain to see
As she moved with her train   to the tumbling breakers.
Many a stately man   stood on the shore
Of the Wendel-Sea.   Swiftly they hurried
Over the border-paths,   band after band.
They loaded the vessels   with byrny and lance,
With men in bucklers,   with battle-sarks,
With man and maid.   O'er the sea-monsters' home
They drove their foaming   deep-flanked ships.
Oft on the waves   the stout wood stood
The blows of the billows.   The ocean roared.

   Never learned I   early or late
Of lady who led   on the ocean-lanes
Fairer band   o'er the paths of the flood.
There might he see   who beheld that sailing
Sea-wood scud   under swelling sails,
Sea-steeds plunge   and break through the billows,
Wave-ships skim.   The warriors bold
Were blithe, and the queen   had joy of the journey.
   When the high-prowed ships   had come to their haven

* Cynewulf's *Elene* 212–65.

Over the ocean   in the Grecian land
They left their vessels   much tossed of the tides,
Their old sea-homes,   at the ocean's shore
Fast at anchor   to await on the waves
The fate of the band,   when the battle-queen
With her troop of warriors   o'er the eastern ways
Should seek them again.   Then was easily seen
Woven mail   on many an eorl
Choicest of blades,   bright battle-byrny,
Visored casque   and fair boar-crest;
There men of war   were on the march,
A convoy of warriors   around their queen.
The stalwart heroes,   heralds of Caesar,
Gaily fared   through the Grecian land,
Men of battle   in shining mail;
And many a gem   in its jeweled setting
Gleamed in that war-host,   the gift of a lord.

St. Andrew's Voyage to Mermedonia *

A Voice from heaven   was heard on earth
In the land of Achaia   where Andrew lodged
Leading the people   in the way of Life.
To the great-hearted hero   the Glory of kings,
Lord of hosts   and Maker of men,
Opened His mind-hoard,   uttered this word:
　"Go forth straightway   faring afar
To seek the coasts   where the Cannibals dwell
With murderous fury   defending their land.
Such is their custom   that in that country
No foreign man   is allowed to live;
If it be that they find one   defenseless there
Deadly torture   and death is his lot.
In bondage of chains   your brother lies
Among that people.   Three nights from now
Through heathen hatred,   smitten with spears,
He shall send forth his soul   on a far journey
Except ere that hour   you haste to help."
　Unto Him promptly   Andrew replied:
"O God of heaven   and Lord of glory,
How can I fare   on so far a course
Over the deep ocean   so soon as Thou sayest?
But this Thine angel   may easily do.
From heaven he sees   the ocean-stretches,
All the swan-road   and the salt sea-streams,
The tumult of waves,   the water-terror,
The ways that lengthen   across wide lands.
I have no friends   in that foreign folk,
I know not the mind   of any man there,
And the ocean-ways   across the cold water
To me are unknown."
　　　　　Then God made answer:

* **Andreas** 167–224; 235–76; 290–326; 343–51; 359–414; 465–536.

28

"Alas! Andrew! that ever your heart
Should be slow to this journey! Slight were the task
For God Almighty to command on earth,
Under the sun, that the city be moved
Unto this country, the stately seat
And all who live there, if the Lord of glory
Decreed it by His word. You may not weary
In this wayfaring, nor waver in heart
If you think to keep covenant, compact with God.
    "At the hour be ready. In performing this errand
Can be no delay. You shall risk your life;
The path shall lead to the power of the foe
Where the crash of battle shall come upon you,
The war-might of heroes and heathen strife.
In the early dawn with the coming of day
At the ocean's margin straightway take ship
And drive through the surges on the cold sea.
My blessing go with you where you go.". . .
    Then Andrew at dawn at the break of day
Over the sand dunes strode to the shore
Keen of courage, his comrades beside him
Tramping the shingle. The ocean resounded,
The combers crashed. The hero rejoiced
When he saw at the sea's edge a broad-beamed boat.
Morning sun came, the brightest of beacons,
Heaven's candle flaming over the flood,
Holy light dawning out of the dark.
He saw there waiting three stately sailors
Geared for the voyage, great-hearted men
In their wave-boat sitting as if come from over sea.
'Twas the Lord Himself, the Leader of men,
Almighty, Eternal, with His angels twain.
They were garbed like mariners, seafaring men,
When they plunge in their keels over cold water
On a far journey o'er the flood's expanse.
    Ready for sea as he stood on the shingle
Andrew bespoke them with hearty hail:

"Sea-crafty men, whence come you sailing
In your ocean-plunger, your peerless bark?
Whence have the sea-streams brought your ship
O'er the tossing main?"
                                    The Almighty made answer
As if He wist not what man it was
Of mortal men who awaited His word,
With whom He held speech on the sandy shore:
"From the Mermedonian folk we have come faring
On a far journey. Over the flood
Dowered with speed our swift sea-stallion,
Our high-prowed courser, carried us on
Along the whale-path until at last
We came to this country urged by the waves
As the wind drove us."
                                    Humble of heart
Andrew made answer: "A boon I would beg
Though I've little to give of treasure or gold,
That you take us along in your tall-sided ship,
Your high-prowed floater, o'er the home of the whale
To the place of that people. And God will reward
Your kindness to us in this ocean-crossing.". . .
    The Prince of angels made reply,
The Saviour of men, from the ship's prow:
"Gladly will we bear you o'er the fishes' bath
To the land that your longing leads you to seek
When you have paid toll, the appointed tribute,
Even as sailors over the ship's side
Are willing to agree."
                                    Then Andrew gave answer
Friendless, penniless, making reply:
"I have no gold, no goodly treasure,
No food or riches or woven rings,
No land or linked jewels, to spur your desire
Or whet your willingness as your words suggest."
    The Sovereign of men where He sat on the gangway
Said unto Andrew o'er the breaking seas:

"How does it happen,   dearest friend,
That lacking money   you would make a voyage
O'er the climbing billows,   past the cold cliffs,
To the far sea-limits?   Have you no food
To bring you comfort,   or clear water
For your refreshment,   on the ocean-flood?
Hard is the life   for one who long
Tries ocean-voyaging."
                                Andrew in answer,
Wise of wit,   his word-hoard unlocked:
"Ill befits it   since God has given you
Food and fortune   and worldly wealth
That you question me thus   with cruel pride
And bitter word.   Better a man
Hail the wayfarer   with humble heart
And kindly spirit,   as Christ once bade,
Our glorious Warden.   We are His thanes,
His chosen champions.   He is True King,
God and Ruler   of celestial glory,
One Lord Eternal   of every created thing," . . .
                                Eternal God answered:
"If, as you say,   you are His servants
Who raised up heaven   high above earth,
And have kept the law   of the Holy Lord,
Gladly will I sail you   over the sea-flood
As you have begged."   Then the heroes brave,
Bold of spirit,   embarked in the ship
And their hearts rejoiced   in the ocean-journey. . . .
    There the saint took seat   near to the Shipman,
Noble beside noble.   Never did I hear
Of fairer vessel   more richly freighted
With stately treasure.   Within it sat
Glorious princes,   and goodly thanes.
And the Powerful Prince,   Eternal and Mighty,
Bade His angel,   His honored thane,
Bring food to nourish   those needy men
On the thronging billows,   that they might the better

31

Endure their lot   on the surging deep.

Then the depths were troubled.   The horn-fish darted
Gliding through ocean;   the gray gull wheeled
Searching for carrion.   The sun grew dark,
A gale arose   and great waves broke;
The sea-streams were stirred.   Halyards were humming,
Sails were drenched.   Sea-terror grew
In the welter of waves.   The thanes were adread
Who sailed with Andrew   on the ocean-stream,
Nor hoped with life   ever to come to land.
Not yet was it known   Who steered their ship
Through the breaking seas.

       Then again the saint
As a loyal thane   thanked his Great Leader
On the ocean-highway,   the oar-stirred sea,
Because his strength   had been stayed with food.

"For this repast   may the Righteous Ruler
Author of life,   and Lord of hosts,
Grant you reward,   and give you for food
The bread of heaven   because you accorded me
Love and good will   on the mountainous waves.
My youthful warriors,   willing thanes,
Are sorely troubled.   The sea resounds,
The surging ocean;   the depths are stirred,
Terribly shaken.   My troop are aghast,
My force of brave followers   deeply dismayed."

Then from the helm   spoke the Maker of men:
"Let us steer the ship,   our floater, to shore
O'er the ocean-main   and there let your men
Tarry on land   until you return."

But straightway the eorls,   strong to endure,
Gave Him answer;   they would not agree
That they should forsake   at the vessel's stem
Their beloved leader   and choose the land:
"If we desert you   whither shall we wander
Lordless and lonely,   lacking all good?
We shall be loathed   in every land,

Hated of all men   where valiant heroes
Sit in assembly   holding debate
Who best has bolstered   his lord in battle
When hand and buckler   were bearing the brunt,
Hacked with swords,   on the field of fate." ...
Then the waves subsided,   the sea's fierce tumult;
The rush of the waters   was turned away.
The saint's heart was happy   that the terror was past.
Sage of counsel   he began to speak,
Wise of wit   he unlocked his word-hoard:
    "Never have I met   more skillful mariner
Or more sea-crafty   than you seem to me;
No stouter sailor,   none sager in counsel
Or wiser in word.   A boon I would beg
Illustrious eorl,   though it's little I have
Of goodly treasure   or gifts of gold.
Gladly would I gain,   O glorious Prince,
Your welcome friendship   if I may win it,
And you shall have grace   and holy hope
In heavenly glory   if you'll graciously share
Your wise counsels   with sea-weary men.
O noble hero,   since the Maker of men,
Our King, has granted you   glory and might,
One art from you   I am eager to learn:
If you will teach me   how you sail your ship,
Your spray-drenched floater,   across the sea.
    "Sixteen voyages   early and late
It has been my lot   to sail in my sea-boat
With freezing hands   as I smote the sea,
The ocean-stream.   This now is another.
Never have I known   one like to you
Of the sons of men   steering over stem.
The roaring billows   beat on the strand;
Full swift is this bark   and most like a bird
Foamy-necked faring   over the waves.
Full well I know   I never have seen
In any sailor   more wondrous sea-craft.

Most like it is   as if on land
The boat stood still   where wind and storm
Could stir it not,   nor breaking billows
Shatter the high prow;   yet it speeds over ocean
Swift under sail.   You yourself are young,
O warden of warriors,   man of the sea;
Not many your winters!   Yet in your mind
You have an eorl's answers;   in any assembly
You have wise understanding   of every word."
  God the Eternal   made answer to Andrew:
"Oft it befalls   on the watery way
That storms arise   as we break through the billows
In ships with sailors,   in our ocean-steeds.
At times it goes hard with us   on the high seas
Even though we survive   the perilous voyage.
But never may Ocean   work ill to any
Against God's will.   He governs life
Who binds the seas,   Who bridles and fetters
The dark flood.   Over every folk
He rules by right   Who raised up the heavens,
With His hands fastened   and fixed their support.
That bright habitation   He filled with bliss,
By His sole might blessed   the abode of angels.
  "Now is it known   and clearly disclosed
That you are His servant   Who sits in glory,
For the sea perceived,   the circle of ocean,
That you had the gift   of the Holy Ghost.
The billows abated,   the tumult of breakers;
The terror was stilled   and the wide-stretching waves.
The seas subsided   when the water saw
That He Whose might   shaped heavenly glory
In His safe-keeping   held you close."

The Voyage of Life *

Now is it most like   as if on ocean
Across cold water   we sail in our keels,
Over the wide sea   in our ocean-steeds,
Faring on in our flood-wood.   Fearful the stream,
The tumult of waters,   whereon we toss
In this feeble world.   Fierce are the surges
On the ocean-lanes.   Hard was our life
Before we made harbor   over the foaming seas.
Then help was vouchsafed   when God's Spirit-Son
Guided us to the harbor of salvation   and granted us grace
That we may understand   over the ship's side
Where to moor our sea-steeds,   our ocean-stallions,
Fast at anchor.   Let us fix our hope
Upon that haven   which the Lord of heaven,
In holiness on high,   has opened by His Ascension.

* *Christ 2* 850–66.

III

RIDDLES AND GNOMIC VERSE

RIDDLES AND GNOMIC VERSE

Included in the Exeter Book and the Cotton MS are excellent examples of two highly conventionalized types of Old English verse: the gatherings of versified riddles, and of versified maxims, or gnomes.

The Old English *Riddles* compose a series of thumbnail sketches of the daily realisms of Old English life. They are in a certain sense a listing of the things with which man's life was woven: the birds and animals of country life, man's food and drink, the tools with which he worked, the armor and weapons with which he fought, his instruments of music. By their range and detailed vividness the *Riddles* supplement the pictures of Old English culture derived from the narrative poems.

It is clear, moreover, that in the shaping of these vernacular *Riddles* there was Latin influence. This was in part exerted by various collections of Latin riddles current among scholars in the eighth century, among others the riddles of Symphosius and Ealdhelm. However, quite aside from any influence of these Latin riddles, there is in the Old English *Riddles* 1, and 2-3, unmistakable evidence of the poet's familiarity with theories of meteorology set forth by Lucretius in the sixth book of the *De Natura,* and by Pliny in the second book of the *Natural History.* It is this Classical theory of meteorology that underlies the sustained imagery of the Old English "Storm" *Riddles.*

The gnomic strain runs like a clearly visible thread through the entire body of Old English poetry. It is found in concentrated form in the *Gnomic Verses,* or *Maxims,* of the Exeter Book and the Cotton MS. But, in addition, many passages in Old English lyric and narrative verse reveal the gnomic mood. The gnome was employed as a brief, pithy, sententious saying, sometimes to set forth proverbial or folk wisdom, sometimes to express generations of keen-eyed observation of nature, sometimes to give folk sanction to a moral, or to define a virtue or vice. A knowledge of the more characteristic gnomes was evidently a part of the literary endowment of an Old English poet.

39

In lines 94-106 of the Exeter Book *Maxims* we find a passage that may possibly be an insertion into a broken text. These lines, coming abruptly as they do, are in themselves notable for preserving a charming vignette of Old English domestic life, a sailor's home-coming. The wife welcomes home her bread-winner, washes his garments stained by the sea, gives him fresh raiment, responds to his love. The fact that the poet specifically refers to the wife as a Frisian, coming as it does without explanation, falls somewhat strangely on the ear. But the Frisians in England came of seafaring stock, and there were Frisians among the sailors who manned King Alfred's navy. There is also evidence suggesting that in the eighth century a Frisian community existed at York.

Riddles *

Anchor

Oft I must strive   with wind and wave,
Battle them both   when under the sea
I feel out the bottom,   a foreign land.
In lying still   I am strong in the strife;
If I fail in that   they are stronger than I
And, wrenching me loose,   soon put me to rout.
They wish to capture   what I must keep.
I can master them both   if my grip holds out,
If the rocks bring succor   and lend support,
Strength in the struggle.   Ask me my name!

Book-Moth

A moth ate a word.   To me it seemed
A marvelous thing   when I learned the wonder
That a worm had swallowed,   in darkness stolen,
The song of a man,   his glorious sayings,
A great man's strength;   and the thieving guest
Was no whit the wiser   for the words it ate.

Cuckoo

In former days   my father and mother
Abandoned me dead,   lacking breath
Or life or being.   Then one began,
A kinswoman kind,   to care for and love me;
Covered me with her clothing,   wrapped me in her raiment
With the same affection   she felt for her own;

* Exeter Book *Riddles* 16, 47, 9, 85, 27, 14, 21, 5, 7, 2-3.

Until by the law   of my life's shaping
Under alien bosom   I quickened with breath.
My foster mother   fed me thereafter
Until I grew sturdy   and strengthened for flight.
Then of her dear ones,   of daughters and sons,
She had the fewer   for what she did.

Fish in River

My house is not quiet,   I am not loud;
But for us God fashioned   our fate together.
I am the swifter,   at times the stronger,
My house more enduring,   longer to last.
At times I rest;   my dwelling still runs;
Within it I lodge   as long as I live.
Should we two be severed,   my death is sure.

Honey-Mead

I am valued by men,   fetched from afar,
Gleaned on the hill-slopes,   gathered in groves,
In dale and on down.   All day through the air
Wings bore me aloft,   and brought me with cunning
Safe under roof.   Men steeped me in vats.
Now I have power   to pummel and bind,
To cast to the earth,   old man and young.
Soon he shall find   who reaches to seize me,
Pits force against force,   that he's flat on the ground,
Stripped of his strength   if he cease not his folly,
Loud in his speech,   but of power despoiled
To manage his mind,   his hands or his feet.
Now ask me my name,   who can bind men on earth
And lay fools low   in the light of day.

Horn

Time was when I   was weapon and warrior;
Now the young hero   hoods me with gold,
And twisted silver.   At times men kiss me.
At times I speak   and summon to battle
Loyal companions.   At times a courser
Bears me o'er marchland.   At times a ship
Bears me o'er billows,   brightly adorned.
At times a fair maiden   fills me with breath;
At times hard and headless   I lie on the board,
Bereft of beauty.   At times I hang
Winsome on wall,   richly embellished,
Where revelers drink.   At times a warrior
Bears me on horse,   a battle adornment,
And I swallow, bright-shining,   the breath from his bosom.
At times with my strains   I summon the heroes
Proudly to wine.   At times I win back
Spoil from the spoiler,   with sounding voice
Put foemen to flight.   Now ask what I'm called.

Plow

My beak is bent downward,   I burrow below;
I grub in the ground   and go as he guides,
My gray, old master,   foe of the forest.
Stoop-shouldered my warder   walks at my back,
Fares through the field,   urges and drives me,
Sows in my track   as I sniff along.
Fetched from the wood,   cunningly fitted,
Brought in a wagon,   I have wondrous skill.
As I go my way   on one side is green;
On the other side plain   is my dark path.
Set through my back   hangs a cunning spike;
Another fixed forward   is fast to my head.
What I tear with my teeth   falls to one side,
If he handles me right   who is my ruler.

43

Shield

A lonely wanderer,   wounded with iron,
I am smitten with war-blades,   sated with strife,
Worn with the sword-edge;   I have seen many battles,
Much hazardous fighting,   oft without hope
Of comfort or help   in the carnage of war
Ere I perish and fall   in the fighting of men.
The leavings of hammers,   the handwork of smiths,
Batter and bite me,   hard-edged and sharp;
The brunt of battle   I am doomed to endure.
In all the folk-stead   no leech could I find
With wort or simple   to heal my wounds;
But day and night   with the deadly blows
The marks of the war-blades   double and deepen.

Wild Swan

My attire is noiseless   when I tread the earth,
Rest in its dwellings   or ride its waters.
At times my pinions   and the lofty air
Lift me high   o'er the homes of men,
And the strength of the clouds   carries me far
High over the folk.   My feathers gay
Sound and make music,   singing shrill,
When no longer I linger   by field or flood,
But soar in air,   a wandering spirit.

Wind

At times I resort,   beyond man's discerning,
Under surging billows   to seek the bottom,
The ocean depths.   Then the sea is shaken,
Convulsed with foam,   and the whale-flood rages
In giant uproar.   The ocean streams
Beat on the shore   and batter the slopes
With rock and sand,   with seaweed and wave.

As I struggle and strain   in the ocean depths
I shake the land   and the vast sea-bottom.
From my watery covering   I cannot forth
Till He grant me freedom   Who guides my way
On every journey.   O wise of wit,
Tell who can draw me   from ocean depths
When the seas grow still   and the waves are calm
Which formerly covered   and cloaked me over.
    Closely at times   my master confines me,
Forces me under   the fruitful plain,
The earth's broad bosom,   and holds me at bay,
Pens my strength   in prison and darkness
Where the earth sits heavy   and hard on my back!
Out of that bondage   escape is barred,
But I wrench and rock   the dwellings of men.
The halls horn-gabled   totter and topple
And over the households   the high walls shake;
The air seems still,   and the sea is silent,
Until from bondage   I burst my way
As He may guide   Who in the beginning
Laid fetters upon me   and bitter bonds;
I may not ever   escape from His power
Who governs my going.
                        At times from above
I must rouse the waters   and stir the waves
And dash on its beaches   the flint-gray flood.
The foaming breakers   fight with the sea-wall,
Hills of water   heave dark on the deep;
Each follows other   in dusky track,
Churning combers   that batter the cliffs
At the edge of the land.   On ship is uproar,
Shouting of sailors.   The steep stone cliffs
Await the sea-war,   the crashing of waves,
As the dashing billows   buffet the headlands.
On ship is dread   of the perilous strife
Lest the ocean bear it   with its burden of souls
To the dreadful hour   when foaming it drives,

Bereft of rudder,   stripped of sailors,
On the shouldering surges.   Then terror shall come
In stormy might   on the sons of men
Which is greater than I.   Whose power shall still it?
    At times I rush   through the clouds that ride me,
Black vessels of rain,   and scatter them far;
At times I join   and gather them in.
The greatest of tumults   resounds over cities,
The loudest of thunders,   when cloud meets cloud
Edge against edge.   Then swift over men
The swart shapes sweat   bright fire and flame,
And dark o'er the hosts   with the greatest of dins
The thunder breaks.   Then the battling hosts
From their bosoms shed   dark showers of rain,
Water from the womb.   They fight their way on,
Dread troop on troop,   and the terror grows,
Dismay of men   and fear in the cities,
When the stalking specters   shoot forth their fire.
    The fool then fears not   the deadly arrows,
But he perishes surely   if God in sooth
Out of the rain   and the roar of the whirlwind
Looses against him   a flying bolt.
But few survive   whom the swift foe strikes,
Reaches with weapon.   I rouse this strife
When I rush in might   with a meeting of clouds
O'er the breast of torrents;   then burst with a roar
The cloud-troops on high.   Then low under heaven
I bow to earth   and load on my back,
At the word of my Lord,   the burden I carry.
    And so at times,   a powerful slave,
I work under earth;   at times I descend
Under surges of ocean;   at times from above
I rouse the sea-streams;   at times I mount up
And whirl the cloud-drift.   Widely I fare
Strong and swift!   Say what I'm called;
Who it is rouses me   when I may not rest;
Who it is stays me   when again I'm still.

Cotton MS. *Maxims*

King must rule kingdom. Cities are seen from afar,
Cunning handwork of giants who inhabit this earth,
Wondrous work of wallstones. Wind is swiftest in air,
Thunder at times is loudest. Great are the glories of Christ.
Wyrd is mightiest, winter is coldest,
Spring is frostiest, longest cold;
Summer is sunniest, sun is hottest,
Autumn most glorious giving to man
The fruits of the year that God brings forth.
Truth is clearest, treasure is dearest,
Gold most precious, age most wise;
Years make prudent who suffers long.
Woe is close clinging; clouds drift by.
Good companions encourage a prince
To glory in battle and giving of gifts.
Eorl must have courage; edge against helm
Survives the sword-play. Hawk on glove
The wild one waits. Wolf in the forest,
Beastly lone-goer. Boar in the wood,
Mighty of tusk. Good man at home
Harvests renown. Spear for the hand
Garnished with gold. Gem for the ring
Ample and wide. Stream in the waves
Shall mix with the sea. Mast for the ship,
The sailyard fastened. Sword on lap,
A lordly blade. In mound dragon bideth,
Old guarder of gold. Fish in water
Must spawn its kind. King in the hall
Must hand out rings. Bear on the heath
Roams old and fierce. River from hills
Flows down flood-gray. Army must be gathered,
A band of the brave. Faith for an eorl,
Wisdom for man. Woods of the world
Must bud with blossoms. Hills of earth

Must gleam with green.   God in heaven
Is judge of deeds.   Door in the hall
Is mouth of the building.   Boss on shield
Is the fingers' guard.   Birds above
Soar in the air.   In deep pool salmon
Swims with the trout.   Showers from heaven
Mingled with wind   sweep over the world.
Thief goes in darkness.   Ghost on the fen
Is alone in the land.   In secret a woman
Will haste to her friend   if she has no wish
To prosper with husband,   purchased with rings.
Sea shall be salt;   water and air
Shall flow in floods   around all lands.
Cattle on earth   shall bear and bring forth.
Stars shine bright   by the Maker's command.
Good against evil;   youth against age;
Life against death;   light against darkness;
Army against army;   foe against foe;
Hostile with hostile   shall always fight
Contending for land   and avenging wrongs.
A wise man must ponder   this world's strife;
Outlaw must hang,   paying the price
That he wronged mankind.

                                God alone knows
Where the soul passes   and all the spirits
Who after their death-days   go before God.
They abide their judgment   in the Father's bosom;
Their future fate   is secret and hid;
God alone knows,   the Saviour Father.
And none returns ever,   hither under roof,
To tell men for truth   of God's decree,
Or the home of the victor-folk,   where He Himself dwells.

Exeter Book *Fates of Men**

Oft it befalls   by the grace of God
That into this world   woman and man
Bring child to birth.   They dress it in colors,
Love it and train it   till time shall come
When its limbs are sturdy   and strong with life.
Father and mother   carry and lead it,
Feed it and clothe it   but God alone knows
What the years may give   for the growing child!
　　To one it happens   in the years of his youth
A woeful ending   carries him off.
A wolf shall devour him,   hoary heath-stepper,
And his mother shall mourn   his going hence.
Little is this   the lot of a man!
　　One hunger shall waste,   one storm shall harry
One spear shall slay,   one battle destroy.
One lives his life   without light of eye,
Only hands for feeling.   One feeble of foot,
Sick of sinew,   shall moan his pain,
Afflicted in spirit   and mourning his fate.
　　One in the forest   from lofty tree
Wingless shall fall;   he shall be in flight
Swinging in air   till no longer he hangs
As fruit from the bough.   He shall fall to earth,
Of soul bereft   at the root of the tree.
His life is ended.   Over far ways
One shall travel,   finding his food,
Facing the perils   of foreign soil,
Having few friends   to offer him welcome,
Everywhere hated,   unhappy at heart,
Everywhere finding   misfortune and woe.
　　One shall swing   on the stretching gallows
Dangling in death   till the body breaks,

* Lines 1–67; 93–8.

The bloody frame,   and the black-coated raven
Picks at the eyeballs,   plucks at the corpse.
Against the outrage   his hands are helpless;
They may not defend   from the winged foe.
Life is vanished,   all feeling fled.
Stark and pallid   he swings on the gallows,
Shrouded in death-mist,   enduring his fate.
His name is accursed.   In the funeral-fire
Flame shall afflict,   red brands consume
One doomed and fated;   his death shall be swift.
The woman shall weep   as she sees the blaze,
The enveloping flame,   devour her son.

   From one on the mead-bench,   a wine-sated man
A quarrelsome drunkard,   the sharp-edged sword
Shall wrest away life;   his words were too rash!
One at the beer-feast   by cupbearer's hand
Grown foolish with mead,   not curbing his mouth,
Shall lose his life   in a wretched brawl,
Shorn of pleasure,   suffering woe;
And men who describe   the drunkard's debauch,
All shall call him   a self-slain man.

   But some shall in youth   by the grace of God
Master misfortune,   in later years
Have joyous heart   and days of gladness,
Feasting with loved ones,   possessing wealth
And all such treasure   as man may hold.
   So in diverse ways   God deals His gifts
Unto every man   through all the earth:
He decides, and settles,   and makes decree,
Giving weal to one,   woe to another. . . .
In wondrous wise   the Warden of hosts
Throughout the world   awards man's fate,
Deciding fortune   for all on earth.
Therefore, let every man   give Him Thanksgiving
For all that His mercy   may allot for men.

Exeter Book *Maxims* *

Frost shall freeze;   fire melt wood;
Earth give blossom;   ice shall bridge
And roof the waters,   wondrously lock
Earth's budding growth.   One shall unbind
The fetters of frost,   Almighty God.
Winter shall pass,   fair weather return,
Sun-hot summer   and restless sea.
Deep slow wave   holds secret longest.
Holly shall be lighted;   dead man's wealth
Among heirs divided.   Honor is best!
  King with wealth   shall purchase his queen
With beakers and bracelets;   both, from the first,
Shall be gracious in giving.   In the lord must grow
Courage and war-might;   the lady shall thrive
Beloved of her people,   a keeper of counsel,
Light of heart   and liberal-handed
With horses and treasure;   at drinking of mead
Before the host   she shall first give greeting
To the leader of warriors,   to hand of her lord
First tendering cup;   knowing wise counsel
To the good of both,   house-owners together.
  Ship shall be nailed,   and buckler bound,
Linden shield light;   loved one is welcome
To Frisian wife   when his boat stands in.
His ship is come   and her sailor home,
Her own food-winner.   She welcomes him in,
Washes his garments   stained by the sea,
Gives him new raiment.   Sweet is the shore
To one whose longing   is urged by love.
A wife should ever   keep faith with her man;
But often she shames him   with evil ways.
Many are steadfast,   many are fickle

* Lines 71–106; 201–4.

Wooing strange men   when their lords are away.
Often the sailor   is long at sea;
But one must look   for the loved one's coming
Awaiting the meeting   one may not speed,
Till the time shall come   that he turns again home,
Alive and hale,   unless ocean trammel,
Or deep sea hold him   with clutching hand. . . .
   Shield shall be ready,   barb on shaft,
Edge on sword   and point on spear!
Stout heart for hero,   helm for the brave,
And ever for faint-heart   scantest of hoards!

IV

CONTINENTAL TRADITION

CONTINENTAL TRADITION

Old English poetry affords evidence of the extent to which Continental tradition persisted in England. It is reflected, of course, in the Scandinavian backgrounds of *Beowulf*, in the poet's retelling of the legends of Sigemund and Finn, and in countless allusions to material of legend and chronicle scattered through the poem. It is found also in details of shorter poems like *Widsith* and *Deor's Lament*, and in the brief poetic fragments that deal with the material of the Waldere and Finnsburg stories.

The Tale of Sigemund in *Beowulf* is in one respect unique, for in Continental legend the great dragon-fight is fought, not by Sigemund, but by his son Sigurd. Moreover, the *Lay of Finn* inset in the poem has little direct relation to the *Finnsburg Fragment* where the theme is the heroic fighting for possession of the great hall. In the *Beowulf Lay* the theme is extended to the tragic issues involved in the bloody racial feud between Danes and Frisians.

Widsith and *Deor's Lament* are poems of minstrel life. Widsith, a strolling singer, tells of his travels, of the great rulers he has known, and the rich gifts he has received. But the allusions cover so many years that no actual Widsith could have visited all the heroic figures he names. Indeed it is a question whether the long "catalogue" of rulers and tribes was a part of the original poem. In many instances, the *Widsith* supplements names and allusions that occur in other Old English poems. Lines 45-49 mention the bitter feud between Danes and Heathobards outlined by Beowulf in his account of his Danish adventures.

The *Lament* of Deor, once court-singer of the Heodenings, tells of his displacement by the minstrel Heorrenda who had supplanted him in his lord's favor and succeeded to the "'landright" Deor once had held. The poem is in strophic arrangement, each strophe rehearsing historic instances of adversity and ending with the refrain: "That evil ended, so also may this!" As Weland and Beadohild, Theodoric and the subjects of Eormanric, had risen above misfortune, so may others also surmount adverse fate.

The two Old English fragments of the *Waldere* are very brief portions of a legend of Walther of Aquitaine. A tenth-century Latin text of this heroic tale, the *Waltharius*, is, except for the Old English fragments, the oldest of surviving versions. The first of the *Waldere* fragments contains a part of Hildegund's exhortation of Walther to do or die in the battle with Gunther. The second fragment includes Walther's challenge of Gunther to come and take, if he can, the corselet that Walther had from his father. If one can judge from these spirited speeches, the *Waldere* in its entirety may well have been an excellent example of the Germanic heroic tale in Old English verse.

Deor's Lament

Weland knew fully   affliction and woe,
Hero unflinching   enduring distress;
Had for companionship   heart-break and longing,
Wintry exile   and anguish of soul,
When Nithhad bound him,   the better man,
Grimly constrained him   with sinewy bonds.
That evil ended.   So also may this!
   Nor was brother's death   to Beadohild
A sorrow as deep   as her own sad plight,
When she knew the weight   of the child in her womb,
But little could know   what her lot might be.
That evil ended.   So also may this!
   Many have heard   of the rape of Hild,
Of her father's affection   and infinite love,
Whose nights were sleepless   with sorrow and grief.
That evil ended.   So also may this!
   For thirty winters   Theodoric held,
As many have known,   the Mæring's stronghold.
That evil ended.   So also may this!
   We have heard of Eormanric's   wolf-like ways,
Widely ruling   the realm of the Goths;
Grim was his menace,   and many a man,
Weighted with sorrow   and presage of woe,
Wished that the end   of his kingdom were come.
That evil ended.   So also may this!
   He who knows sorrow,   despoiled of joys,
Sits heavy of mood;   to his heart it seemeth
His measure of misery   meeteth no end.
Yet well may he think   how oft in this world
The wise Lord varies   His ways to men,
Granting wealth and honor   to many an eorl,
To others awarding   a burden of woe.

And so I can sing   of my own sad plight
Who long stood high   as the Heodenings' bard,
Deor my name,   dear to my lord.
Mild was my service   for many a winter,
Kindly my king   till Heorrenda came
Skillful in song   and usurping the land-right
Which once my gracious lord   granted to me.
That evil ended.   So also may this!

Widsith, the Minstrel *

Widsith spoke,   his word-hoard unlocked,
Who most had traveled   of men on earth
Among many peoples,   and prospered in hall
With splendid treasure.   His forebears sprang
From the Myrging tribe.   In his earliest travels
With Ealhild he went,   fair weaver of peace,
From the East out of Angle   to Eormanric's home,
Who was prince of the Goths,   fierce breaker of pledges.
Many a tale   he told of his travels:
   "Much have I learned   of the rulers of men!
A prince must live   by custom and law,
Each after other   ruling the realm,
Who wishes his power   to prosper and thrive.
Of them was Hwala   a while the best,
And Alexander   greatest of all
Of the race of men;   he prospered most
Of all I have heard of   over the earth.
Attila ruled the Huns,   Eormanric the Goths,
Becca the Banings,   Gifica the Burgundians;
Caesar ruled the Greeks,   Caelic the Finns,
Hagena the Holmrygir,   Heoden the Glomman;
Witta ruled the Swabians,   Wada the Hælsings,
Meaca the Myrgings,   Mearchealf the Hundings;
Theodoric ruled the Franks,   Thyle the Rondings,
Breca the Brondings,   Billing the Wernas;
Oswine ruled the Eowas,   Gefwulf the Jutes,
Finn, son of Folcwalda,   the Frisian folk.
Sighere longest   governed the Sea Danes;
Hnæf ruled the Hocings,   Helm the Wulfings. . .
   "I have fared through many   a foreign land

* *Widsith* 1–29; 50–58; 70–74; 88–108; 135–43.

Over spacious earth,   knowing weal and woe,
Bereft of my kinsmen,   far from my folk,
Widely wandering   over the world.
Many a song   and many a story
I can tell in the mead-hall,   recounting to men
How princes and nobles   graced me with gifts.
I was with the Huns,   and with the Hrethgoths,
With Swedes I was, and with Geats,   and with South-Danes. ...
    "I was in Italy also   with Ælfwine
Who of all mankind   as ever I heard
Had the easiest hand   in the earning of praise,
And the readiest heart   in the giving of rings,
The shining jewels,   Eadwine's son. ...
    "I was with Eormanric,   and all the while
The king of the Goths   was gracious and kind.
He gave me a ring,   the ruler of cities,
Worth six hundred sceats   counted in cost
Of shilling pieces   of smelted gold.
To Eadgils I gave it,   my gracious lord,
To requite his kindness   when home I came.
For the lord of the Myrgings   had granted me land,
The holding and home   of my father before me.
    "And Ealhild also   gave me a ring,
The fair folk-queen,   the daughter of Eadwine.
To many a people   her praise I published
Whenever in song   my task was to tell
Of a gold-decked queen   most kind under heaven,
Best and most gracious   in giving of gifts.
There Scilling and I   in echoing strains
Before our dear lord   lifted our songs.
Loud to the harp   the lay resounded;
And many a noble   who knew aright
Said he had never   heard better song." ...
    Widely they wander,   as Fate may guide,
The strolling singers   who roam the world

Telling their need,   returning their thanks,
And always finding,   or south or north,
Some great one skilled   in knowledge of song
Who is open-handed   in giving of gifts,
Who seeks for honor   and strives for fame
Till all things vanish,   light and life
Passing together.   He who earns praise
Has under heaven   the greatest glory.

The Tale of Sigemund *

Old tales were told   of Sigemund's daring,
War-deeds of the Wælsing,   his wanderings wide,
Much of unknown,   the merciless feuds
The sons of men   no longer remembered,
Save Fitela only,   as uncle to nephew
Had told these tales   when they fought together,
Battle-comrades   in bitter fight.
Many a monster   they slew with the sword.
   After Sigemund's death   his glory increased
For the keen in battle   had killed the Worm,
The treasure-guarder.   Beneath gray rock
The valiant hero   had ventured alone
On the fearful deed.   Nor was Fitela with him.
To him it was granted   his good sword pierced
The wondrous Worm   till it stood in the wall,
The lordly iron.   The Dragon died.
The hero's valor   had won the treasure,
The hoard to enjoy   as his heart might wish.
He loaded his sea-boat,   bore to its bosom
Shining treasure,   the son of Wæls.
The surge of its fire   consumed the Worm.
   He was of heroes   most famous afar
For daring deeds,   the defender of fighters.
He prospered greatly   long ago!

* *Beowulf* 874–900.

The Lay of Finn *

Then Hrothgar's minstrel   rehearsed the lay
Of the sons of Finn   when the slaughter befell them:
Hnæf of the Scyldings,   the Half-Dane hero,
Was doomed to death   in the Frisian fight.
Nor could Hildeburh praise   the faith of the Jutes!
She was blameless, shorn   of brothers and sons
In the play of shields,   deprived of beloved
Fated and fallen,   wounded with spears.
Her heart was heavy.   Not for little Hoc's daughter
Mourned their death   at the dawning of day
When she saw under sky   the slaughter of kinsmen
Where once she had known   life's fairest delights.
    War laid them low,   the thanes of Finn,
Save only a few.   Nor could he fight Hengest
Or harry his host;   and they offered a truce:
A hall and high-seat,   a sharing of rights
With the sons of the Jutes;   and that Folcwalda's son
Would honor the Danes,   in the giving of gifts,
With rings and gold   as he gave to the Frisians
To gladden their hearts   on benches in hall.
Both trusted the terms of the truce.   And Finn
Swore oaths to Hengest   forceful and firm
He would rule his remnant   by councils' decree;
And that no man ever   by act or by word
Would break the truce,   or mention with malice
That they who were lordless   were fated to follow
The lord who had killed   their former king;
And if ever a Frisian   should fan the feud
With insolent speech   the sword would avenge it.
    Then the pyre was prepared,   gold drawn from the hoard,

* *Beowulf* 1066–1159.

And the Scylding leader   was laid on the bier.
In the funeral flame   was easily seen
Blood-stained byrny   and golden swine,
Gilded boar-helm   hard from the hammer,
And many a warrior   fated with wounds
And fallen in battle.   Hildeburh bade
That her son be laid   on the bier of Hnæf
And his body burned   at his uncle's shoulder.
The lady lamented   with mournful dirge.
The hero was placed   on the funeral pyre;
The greatest of bale-fires   rolled with a roar
To the skies above   at the burial barrow.
Then heads were melted   and wounds gaped wide;
Blood flowed, and flame,   most greedy of spirits,
Swallowed all battle had taken   of both their peoples.
    Their glory was gone.   The warriors went to their homes,
Bereft of friends,   returning to Friesland
To city and stronghold.   But Hengest remained
Abiding unhappy with Finn.   Though he longed for home,
He could not sail on the sea   his ring-stemmed ship.
The billows boiled with storm   and strove with the wind;
Winter locked ocean   with bonds of ice,
Till a new Spring shone   on the dwellings of men,
As still it does,   the sunny and shining days
That ever observe their season.   The winter was gone
And fair was the bosom of earth.   Then the exile
Longed to be gone,   the guest from his dwelling.
But his mind was more on revenge   than on sailing the sea,
Assault on the Jutes   and a storming with sword.
He spurned it not when Hunlafing   laid in his lap
His battle-flasher,   the best of blades.
Well known was its war-edge   to men of the Jutes!
    Then death by the sword befell Finn,   the fierce-hearted,
When Oslaf and Guthlaf brooded   on the grim attack,
After the sea-journey sorrow   and weight of woe,

And they could not bridle the fury   within their breasts.
The hall was strewn with bodies   and red with blood;
Finn was killed,   the king with his men,
And the queen was taken.   The Scyldings carried to ship
All the wealth of the king,   such jewels and gems
As they found in the home of Finn.   And the fairest of women
They bore over sea-paths   back to the Danes
Back to her home,   and her own dear people.

The Battle of Finnsburg

. . ."are the horns of the hall on fire?"
Then Hnæf made answer,   the battle-young king:
"This is no dawn from the East,   nor flying dragon,
Nor fire burning   the horns of this hall,
But men in armor;   the eagle shall scream,
The gray wolf howl   and the war-wood whistle,
Shield answer shaft.   Now shines the moon
Through scudding cloud.   Dire deeds are come
Bringing hard battle   and bitter strife.
Awake, my warriors,   seize your shields;
Fight like men   in the front of battle;
Be bold of mood,   be mindful of valor!"
    Then sprang up many   a gold-decked thane,
Girding on sword.   The great-hearted warriors,
Sigeferth and Eaha,   drew their swords,
Springing to one door;   Ordlaf and Guthlaf
Guarded the other   while Hengest himself
Followed them close.   Garulf urged Guthere
In the first onset   not so freely
At the door of the hall   to hazard his life,
Where the bold in battle   would wrench it away.
But the brave-hearted hero,   for all to hear,
Called to know   who was holding the door?
"Sigeferth is my name (said he);   I am prince of the Secgas
A wide-known wanderer;   I have borne many blows
In many fierce battles.   At my hand you can have
Whatever you wish   to have from me."
    Then in the hall   was the sound of slaughter,
Boat-shaped shield   upraised by the brave.
Bucklers burst;   hall-boards resounded;
Till Garulf in fighting   was first to fall,
The son of Guthlaf,   with many a good man,
Bodies of dying.   Swarthy and dark
The ravens were circling.   There was flashing of swords

As if all Finnsburg   were blazing with fire.

   Never have I heard   of worthier warriors
Who bore themselves better   in brunt of war,
Or of finer service   more fitly paid
Than those young heroes   rendered to Hnæf.
Five days they fought   and none of them fell,
His faultless comrades,   and they held the doors.

   Then a wounded warrior   turned him away,
Said his byrny was broken   his war-gear weak,
His helmet pierced.   The prince of the people
Asked how the warriors   survived their wounds,
Or which of the young men. . . .

Waldere 1 *

                ... heard him gladly.
"Weland's work surely   can never weaken
For any man   who can hold the hard blade,
Wield the sword, Mimming.   Often in war
Wounded and bloody   man after man
Fell in the fray.   Now let not thy strength,
Soldier of Attila,   or thy valor fail.
    "Now the day has come   when thou shalt accomplish
One of two: either lose thy life,
Or win long fame,   O Ælfhere's son,
Among all mankind.   Not at all, my beloved,
Can I say that ever   in play of swords
I saw you shamefully   shun the battle,
Or turn to the wall   to protect your life,
Though many a hard blade   hacked at your byrny.
But always further   you forced the fighting
Time beyond measure;   I feared for your fate
Lest all too boldly   you pressed to the battle,
The bloody encounter   in clash of war.
    "Now honor your name   with deeds of note
While God is gracious   and grants you strength.
Fear not for the blade!   The best of weapons
Was surely given   to save us both.
With its edge you shall beat down   Guthhere's boast
Who wickedly started   this bitter strife,
Refused the sword,   and the shining casket,
And wealth of jewels.   With never a gem
He shall leave the battle,   return to his lord,
His ancient homeland,   or here shall he sleep
If he ..."

* Fragment 1, 1–32.

Waldere 2 *

Waldere addressed him,   the warrior brave;
He held in his hand   his comfort in battle,
War-blade in his grip,   and uttered these words:
"Lo! grimly you hoped   Burgundian lord,
That the hand of Hagen   would help in the fray
And hinder my fighting;   try and take, if you dare,
Battle-worn though I be,   my good gray byrny.
Here it lies on my shoulders,   shining with gold,
Ælfhere's heirloom   of ample front,
A peerless corselet   for prince's wear
When hand guards body   and frame from the foe!
It fails me not   when the false and unfriendly
Renew their tricks,   and attack me with swords
As ye have done."

* Fragment 2, 11–24.

Charm for a Sudden Stitch

*(For a sudden stitch: feverfew, and the
red nettle that grows into the house,
and plantain; boil in butter.)*

Loud were they, loud,   as they rode o'er the hill;
Fierce was their mood   as they rode through the land;
Shield thee now   and be healed of this hurt;
   Out little spear,   if in here it be!
I lifted up linden,   my shining shield,
When the mighty women   mustered their strength,
And sped against me   their screaming spears.
Back again   I'll give them another,
A flying arrow   full in the front;
   Out little spear,   if in here it be!
Sat a smith   a little knife shaping,
Most cutting of irons,   wondrous keen;
   Out little spear,   if in here it be!
Six smiths sat   slaughter-spears shaping;
   Out spear!   Be not in, spear!
If here within   be a whit of iron,
The work of witches,   it shall melt away.
Be thou shot in fell,   or shot in flesh,
Or shot in blood,   or shot in bone,
Or shot in limb   be thy life unscathed!
Were it shot of Esa,   or shot of elves,
Or shot of hags,   now will I help thee!
This—to heal Esa-shot;   This—to heal elf-shot;
This—to heal hag-shot;   So will I help thee!
Fly, witch, to the wood;   healed be this hurt!
So help thee the Lord!

Charm for Unfruitful Land

Erce, Erce, Erce,   Mother of earth,
May the All-Wielder,   Lord Eternal,
Give flourishing acres   of sprouting shoots,
Acres bountiful   bringing to harvest
Tall stalks   and shining growth,
Acres of broad   harvest of barley,
Acres of white   harvest of wheat,
And all the harvests   of earth!
May Eternal God   and His saints in heaven
Defend earth's growth   from every foe
That it may be shielded   from every evil,
And every sorcery   sowed through the land.
Now I pray the All-Wielder   who shaped the world
That there be no woman   so wagging of tongue,
Nor any man   so cunning of craft,
That may ever pervert   the words thus spoken!

(Then take the plough, and turn the first furrow, and say:)

Be healed, O Earth,   O Mother of men,
Be hale and growing   by grace of God:
Be filled with food   for the use of men!

*(Then take meal of every kind and bake a loaf as broad
as the inside of the hand, and knead it with milk and with
holy water, and lay it under the first furrow. Then say:)*

Acre grow full   with food for men
Brightly blowing.   Be thou blessed
In the name of the Holy One,   Maker of heaven,
And Maker of earth   whereon we live.
May God, Who made ground,   grant sprouting gifts
That each kind of grain   may grow for men.

V

BEOWULF'S LAST BATTLE

BEOWULF'S LAST BATTLE

Of unknown authorship, the *Beowulf* is the outstanding poetic achievement of its age. It is a poem of cultivated craftsmanship and Christian spirit. Sophisticated rather than primitive, its style suggests the influence of literary tradition. Its lines move with an epic dignity of speech and action which may reflect a debt to Vergil in an age when the *Aeneid* was well known to scholars.

The material of the poem is largely Scandinavian. Beowulf's slaying of the hall-haunting Grendel and the troll-wife, his mother, has analogues in various versions of the Continental "Bear's Son" folk-tale. Names of early Swedish kings, mentioned in *Beowulf*, correspond to names in the *Ynglinga Tál*. Incidents relating to the ruling house of the Danes have their analogues in the *Skjoldungasaga*. Woven into this material are references to the savage feuds of the Continental tribes, the Danes and Frisians, Danes and Heathobards, Geats and Swedes.

It is not possible to trace the dragon-fight in *Beowulf* to specific sources or analogues. However, the guarding of burial treasure by a dragon is in accord with the nature of dragons as set forth in the *Gnomic Verses* of the Cotton MS: "The dragon bideth in the grave-mound, old guarder of gold." The treasure buried in the *Beowulf* grave-mound is described in a vivid passage, 2232-70, that is worthy of comparison with the elegiac lines of *The Wanderer*, and *The Ruin*.

The fire-dragon of *Beowulf*, roused by the theft of a flagon from its hoard, ravaged the kingdom with flame. Beowulf and eleven followers went out against him. But Beowulf's comrades, terrified at the dragon's first onset, fled from the battle. Only the youthful Wiglaf remained to fight beside his lord, and his curse upon the cowards is one of the finest expressions of *comitatus* loyalty in Old English verse. In its third rush the dragon fastened its fangs in Beowulf's throat. The king had received his death-wound and his fast failing strength barely sufficed, with Wiglaf's help, to strike down the beast.

75

There is a climactic grandeur in the final scenes of *Beowulf* which illustrates well the author's poetic skill. He describes no popular rejoicing over the killing of the dragon, or the recovery of the rich treasure hoard. The dragon's huge carcass is tumbled over the cliff-edge into the sea, and the treasure is reburied in Beowulf's barrow. An immeasurable disaster had befallen the Geats. Beowulf had ruled them long with strength and wisdom, a settler of ancient feuds, a preserver of peace. The Messenger who brought the news of his death rehearsed the bloody battle against the Swedes at Ravenswood, and chanted his foreboding of evil days to come. A shadow of doom darkened over the people. The old order was ending with the funeral flames and the sound of a people's sorrow for the passing of a great king.

The Fire-Dragon and the Treasure *

It later befell   in the years that followed
After Hygelac sank   in the surges of war,
And the sword slew Heardred   under his shield
When the Battle-Scylfings,   those bitter fighters,
Invaded the land   of the victor-folk
Overwhelming Hereric's nephew   in war,
That the kingdom came   into Beowulf's hand.
    For fifty winters   he governed it well,
Aged and wise   with the wisdom of years,
Till a fire-drake flying   in darkness of night
Began to ravage   and work his will.
On the upland heath   he guarded a hoard,
A stone barrow lofty.   Under it lay
A path concealed   from the sight of men.
There a thief broke in   on the heathen treasure,
Laid hand on a flagon   all fretted with gold,
As the dragon discovered,   though cozened in sleep
By the pilferer's cunning.   The people soon found
That the mood of the dragon   was roused to wrath!
    Not at all with intent,   of his own free will,
Did he ravish the hoard,   who committed the wrong;
But in dire distress   the thrall of a thane,
A guilty fugitive   fleeing the lash,
He forced his way in.   There a horror befell him!
Yet the wretched exile   escaped from the dragon,
Swift in retreat   when the terror arose.
A flagon he took.   There, many such treasures
Lay heaped in that earth-hall   where the owner of old
Had carefully hidden   the precious hoard,
The countless wealth   of a princely clan.
    Death came upon them   in days gone by

---

* *Beowulf* 2200–2354.

And he who lived longest,   the last of his line,
Guarding the treasure   and grieving for friend,
Deemed it his lot   that a little while only
He too might hold   that ancient hoard.
A barrow new-built   near the ocean billows
Stood cunningly fashioned   beneath the cliff;
Into the barrow   the ring-warden bore
The princely treasure,   the precious trove
Of golden wealth,   and these words he spoke:
"Keep thou, O Earth,   what men could not keep,
This costly treasure   —it came from thee!
Baleful slaughter   has swept away,
Death in battle,   the last of my blood;
They have lived their lives;   they have left the mead-hall.
Now I have no one   to wield the sword,
No one to polish   the plated cup,
The precious flagon;   the host is fled.
The hard-forged helmet   fretted with gold
Shall be stripped of its inlay;   the burnishers sleep
Whose charge was to brighten   the battle-masks.
Likewise the corselet   that countered in war
Mid clashing of bucklers   the bite of the sword—
Corselet and warrior   decay into dust;
Mailed coat and hero   are moveless and still.
No mirth of gleewood,   no music of harp,
No good hawk swinging   in flight through the hall;
No swift steed stamps   in the castle yard;
Death has ravished   an ancient race."
So sad of mood   he bemoaned his sorrow,
Lonely and sole   survivor of all,
Restless by day   and wretched by night
Till the clutch of death   caught at his heart.

   Then the goodly treasure   was found unguarded
By the venomous dragon   enveloped in flame,
The old naked night-foe   flying in darkness,
Haunting the barrows;   a bane that brings

A fearful dread   to the dwellers of earth.
His wont is to hunt out   a hoard under ground
And guard heathen gold,   growing old with the years.
But no whit for that   is his fortune more fair!

For three hundred winters   this waster of peoples
Held the huge treasure-hall   under the earth
Till the robber aroused him   to anger and rage,
Stole the rich beaker   and bore to his master,
Imploring his lord   for a compact of peace.
So the hoard was robbed   and its riches plundered;
To the wretch was granted   the boon that he begged;
And his liege-lord first   had view of the treasure,
The ancient work   of the men of old.

Then the worm awakened   and war was kindled,
The rush of the monster   along the rock,
When the fierce one found   the tracks of the foe;
He had stepped too close   in his stealthy cunning
To the dragon's head.   But a man undoomed
May endure with ease   disaster and woe
If he has His favor   who wields the world.
Swiftly the fire-drake   sought through the plain
The man who wrought him   this wrong in his sleep.
Inflamed and savage   he circled the mound,
But the waste was deserted;   no man was in sight.

The worm's mood was kindled   to battle and war;
Time and again   he returned to the barrow
Seeking the treasure-cup.   Soon he was sure
That a man had plundered   the precious gold.
Enraged and restless   the hoard-warden waited
The gloom of evening.   The guard of the mound
Was swollen with anger;   the fierce one resolved
To requite with fire   the theft of the cup.
Then the day was sped   as the worm desired;
Lurking no longer   within his wall
He sallied forth   surrounded with fire,
Encircled with flame.   For the folk of the land

79

The beginning was dread   as the ending was grievous
That came so quickly   upon their lord.

  Then the baleful dragon   belched fire and flame,
Burned the bright dwellings;   the glow of the blaze
Filled hearts with horror.   The hostile flier
Was minded to leave there   nothing alive.
From near and from far   the war of the dragon,
The might of the monster,   was widely revealed
So that all could see   how the ravaging scather
Hated and humbled   the Geatish folk.
Then he hastened back   ere the break of dawn
To his secret den   and the spoil of gold.
He had compassed the land   with a flame of fire,
A blaze of burning;   he trusted the wall,
The sheltering mound,   and the strength of his might.
But his trust betrayed him!   The terrible news
Was brought to Beowulf,   told for a truth,
That his home was consumed   in the surges of fire,
The goodly dwelling   and throne of the Geats.

  The heart of the hero   was heavy with anguish,
The greatest of sorrows;   in his wisdom he weened
He had grievously angered   the Lord Everlasting,
Blamefully broken   the ancient law.
Dark thoughts stirred   in his surging bosom,
Welled in his breast,   as was not his wont.
The flame of the dragon   had leveled the fortress,
The people's stronghold   washed by the wave.
But the king of warriors,   prince of the Weders,
Exacted an ample   revenge for it all.
The lord of warriors   and leader of eorls
Bade work him of iron   a wondrous shield,
Knowing full well   that wood could not serve him
Nor linden defend him   against the flame.
The stalwart hero   was doomed to suffer
The destined end   of his days on earth;
Likewise the worm,   though for many a winter

He had held his watch   o'er the wealth of the hoard.
  The ring-prince scorned   to assault the dragon
With a mighty army,   or host of men.
He feared not the combat,   nor counted of worth
The might of the worm,   his courage and craft,
Since often aforetime,   beset in the fray,
He had safely issued   from many an onset,
Many a combat   and, crowned with success,
Purged of evil   the hall of Hrothgar
And crushed out Grendel's   loathsome kin. . . .

Beowulf and Wiglaf Slay the Dragon *

For the last time Beowulf   uttered his boast:
"I came in safety   through many a conflict
In the days of my youth;   and now even yet,
Old as I am,   I will fight this feud,
Do manful deeds,   if the dire destroyer
Will come from his cavern   to meet my sword."
The king for the last time   greeted his comrades,
Bold helmet-bearers   and faithful friends:
   "I would bear no sword   nor weapon to battle
With the evil worm,   if I knew how else
I could close with the fiend,   as I grappled with Grendel.
From the worm I look   for a welling of fire,
A belching of venom,   and therefore I bear
Shield and byrny.   Not one foot's space
Will I flee from the monster,   the ward of the mound.
It shall fare with us both   in the fight at the wall
As Fate shall allot,   the lord of mankind.
Though bold in spirit,   I make no boast
As I go to fight   with the flying serpent.
Clad in your corselets   and trappings of war,
By the side of the barrow   abide you to see
Which of us twain   may best after battle
Survive his wounds.   Not yours the adventure,
Nor the mission of any,   save mine alone,
To measure his strength   with the monstrous dragon
And play the part   of a valiant eorl.
By deeds of daring   I'll gain the gold
Or death in battle   shall break your lord."
   Then the stalwart rose   with his shield upon him,
Bold under helmet,   bearing his sark
Under the stone-cliff;   he trusted the strength
Of his single might.   Not so does a coward!

* *Beowulf* 2510–2614; 2631–2711.

He who survived   through many a struggle,
Many a combat   and crashing of troops,
Saw where a stone-arch   stood by the wall
And a gushing stream   broke out from the barrow.
Hot with fire   was the flow of its surge,
Nor could any abide   near the hoard unburned,
Nor endure its depths,   for the flame of the dragon.
   Then the lord of the Geats   in the grip of his fury
Gave shout of defiance;   the strong-heart stormed.
His voice rang out   with the rage of battle,
Resounding   under the hoary stone.
Hate was aroused;   the hoard-warden knew
'Twas the voice of a man.   No more was there time
To sue for peace;   the breath of the serpent,
A blast of venom,   burst from the rock.
The ground resounded;   the lord of the Geats
Under the barrow   swung up his shield
To face the dragon;   the coiling foe
Was gathered to strike   in the deadly strife.
The stalwart hero   had drawn his sword,
His ancient heirloom   of tempered edge;
In the heart of each   was fear of the other!
   The shelter of kinsmen   stood stout of heart
Under towering shield   as the great worm coiled;
Clad in his war-gear   he waited the rush.
In twisting folds   the flame-breathing dragon
Sped to its fate.   The shield of the prince
For a lesser while guarded   his life and his body
Than heart had hoped.   For the first time then
It was not his portion   to prosper in war;
Fate did not grant him . glory in battle!
Then lifted his arm   the lord of the Geats
And smote the worm   with his ancient sword
But the brown edge failed   as it fell on bone,
And cut less deep   than the king had need
In his sore distress.   Savage in mood
The ward of the barrow   countered the blow

With a blast of fire;   wide sprang the flame.
The ruler of Geats   had no reason to boast;
His unsheathed iron,   his excellent sword,
Had weakened as it should not,   had failed in the fight.
It was no easy journey   for Ecgtheow's son
To leave this world   and against his will
Find elsewhere a dwelling!   So every man shall
In the end give over   this fleeting life.

 Not long was the lull.   Swiftly the battlers
Renewed their grapple.   The guard of the hoard
Grew fiercer in fury.   His venomous breath
Beat in his breast.   Enveloped in flame
The folk-leader suffered   a sore distress.
No succoring band   of shoulder-companions,
No sons of warriors   aided him then
By valor in battle.   They fled to the forest
To save their lives;   but a sorrowful spirit
Welled in the breast   of one of the band.
The call of kinship   can never be stilled
In the heart of a man   who is trusty and true.

 His name was Wiglaf,   Weohstan's son,
A prince of the Scylfings,   a peerless thane,
Ælfhere's kinsman;   he saw his king
Under his helmet   smitten with heat.
He thought of the gifts   which his lord had given,
The wealth and the land   of the Wægmunding line
And all the folk-rights   his father had owned;
Nor could he hold back,   but snatched up his buckler,
His linden shield   and his ancient sword,
Heirloom of Eanmund,   Ohthere's son,
Whom Weohstan slew   with the sword in battle,
Wretched and friendless   and far from home. . . .

 Wiglaf spoke   in sorrow of soul,
With bitter reproach   rebuking his comrades:
"I remember the time,   as we drank in the mead-hall,
When we swore to our lord   who bestowed these rings
That we would repay   for the war-gear and armor,

The hard swords and helmets,   if need like this
Should ever befall him.   He chose us out
From all the host   for this high adventure,
Deemed us worthy   of glorious deeds,
Gave me these treasures,   regarded us all
As high-hearted bearers   of helmet and spear—
Though our lord himself,   the shield of his people,
Thought single-handed   to finish this feat,
Since of mortal men   his measure was most
Of feats of daring   and deeds of fame.
"Now is the day   that our lord has need
Of the strength and courage   of stalwart men.
Let us haste to succor   his sore distress
In the horrible heat   and the merciless flame.
God knows I had rather   the fire should enfold
My body and limbs   with my gold-friend and lord.
Shameful it seems   that we carry our shields
Back to our homes   ere we harry the foe
And ward the life   of the Weder king.
Full well I know   it is not his due
That he alone,   of the host of the Geats,
Should suffer affliction   and fall in the fight.
One helmet and sword,   one byrny and shield,
Shall serve for us both   in the storm of strife."
    Then Wiglaf dashed   through the deadly reek
In his battle-helmet   to help his lord.
Brief were his words: "Beloved Beowulf, ·
Summon your strength,   remember the vow
You made of old   in the years of youth
Not to allow   your glory to lessen
As long as you lived.   With resolute heart,
And dauntless daring,   defend your life
With all your force.   I fight at your side!"
    Once again the worm,   when the words were spoken,
The hideous foe   in a horror of flame,
Rushed in rage   at the hated men.
Wiglaf's buckler   was burned to the boss

In the billows of fire;   his byrny of mail
Gave the young hero   no help or defense.
But he stoutly pressed on   under shield of his kinsman
When his own was consumed   in the scorching flame.

   Then the king once more   was mindful of glory,
Swung his great sword-blade   with all his might
And drove it home   on the dragon's head.
But Nægling broke,   it failed in the battle,
The blade of Beowulf,   ancient and gray.
It was not his lot   that edges of iron
Could help him in battle;   his hand was too strong,
Overtaxed, I am told,   every blade with its blow.
Though he bore a wondrous   hard weapon to war,
No whit the better   was he thereby!

   A third time then   the terrible scather,
The monstrous dragon   inflamed with the feud,
Rushed on the king   when the opening offered,
Fierce and flaming;   fastened its fangs
In Beowulf's throat;   he was bloodied with gore;
His life-blood streamed   from the welling wound.

   As they tell the tale,   in the king's sore need
His shoulder-companion   showed forth his valor,
His craft and courage,   and native strength.
To the head of the dragon   he paid no heed,
Though his hand was burned   as he helped his king.
A little lower   the stalwart struck
At the evil beast,   and his blade drove home
Plated and gleaming.   The fire began
To lessen and wane.   The king of the Weders
Summoned his wits;   he drew the dagger
He wore on his corselet,   cutting and keen
And slit asunder   the worm with the blow.
So they felled the foe   and wrought their revenge;
The kinsmen together   had killed the dragon.
So a man should be   when the need is bitter!
That was the last fight   Beowulf fought;
That was the end   of his work in the world.

Beowulf's Death *

The wound which the dragon   had dealt him began
To swell and burn;   and soon he could feel
The baneful venom   inflaming his breast.
The wise, old warrior   sank down by the wall
And stared at the work   of the giants of old,
The arches of stone   and the standing columns
Upholding the ancient   earth-hall within.
His loyal thane,   the kindest of comrades,
Saw Beowulf bloody   and broken in war;
In his hands bore water   and bathed his leader,
And loosened the helm   from his dear lord's head.
   Beowulf spoke,   though his hurt was sore,
The wounds of battle   grievous and grim.
Full well he weened   that his life was ended,
And all the joy   of his years on earth;
That his days were done,   and Death most near:
"My armor and sword   I would leave to my son
Had Fate but granted,   born of my body,
An heir to follow me   after I'm gone.
For fifty winters   I've ruled this realm
And never a lord   of a neighboring land
Dared strike with terror   or seek with sword.
In my life I abode   by the lot assigned,
Kept well what was mine,   courted no quarrels,
Swore no false oaths.   And now for all this
Though my hurt is grievous,   my heart is glad.
When life leaves body,   the Lord of mankind
Cannot lay to my charge   the killing of kinsmen!
Go quickly, dear Wiglaf,   to gaze on the gold
Beneath the hoar stone.   The dragon lies still
In the sleep of death,   despoiled of his hoard.
Make haste that my eyes   may behold the treasure,

* Beowulf 2711–2891.

87

The gleaming jewels,   the goodly store,
And, glad of the gold,   more peacefully leave
The life and the realm   I have ruled so long."
    Then Weohstan's son,   as they tell the tale,
Clad in his corselet   and trappings of war,
Hearkened at once   to his wounded lord.
Under roof of the barrow   he broke his way.
Proud in triumph   he stood by the seat,
Saw glittering jewels   and gold on the ground,
The den of the dragon,   the old dawn-flier,
And all the wonders   along the walls.
Great bowls and flagons   of bygone men
Lay all unburnished   and barren of gems,
Many a helmet   ancient and rusted,
Many an arm-ring   cunningly wrought.
Treasure and gold,   though hid in the ground,
Override man's wishes,   hide them who will!
High o'er the hoard   he beheld a banner,
Greatest of wonders,   woven with skill,
All wrought of gold;   its radiance lighted
The vasty ground   and the glittering gems.
But no sign of the worm!   The sword-edge had slain him.
    As I've heard the tale,   the hero unaided
Rifled those riches   of giants of old,
The hoard in the barrow,   and heaped in his arms
Beakers and platters,   picked what he would
And took the banner,   the brightest of signs.
The ancient sword   with its edge of iron
Had slain the worm   who watched o'er the wealth,
In the midnight flaming,   with menace of fire
Protecting the treasure   for many a year
Till he died the death.   Then Wiglaf departed
In haste returning   enriched with spoil.
He feared, and wondered   if still he would find
The lord of the Weders   alive on the plain,
Broken and weary   and smitten with wounds.
With his freight of treasure   he found the prince,

His dear lord, bloody   and nigh unto death.
With water he bathed him   till words broke forth
From the hoard of his heart   and, aged and sad,
Beowulf spoke,   as he gazed on the gold:
   "For this goodly treasure   whereon I gaze
I give my thanks   to the Lord of all,
To the Prince of glory,   Eternal God,
Who granted me grace   to gain for my people
Such dower of riches   before my death.
I gave my life   for this golden hoard.
Heed well the wants,   the need of my people;
My hour is come,   and my end is near.
Bid warriors build,   when they burn my body,
A stately barrow   on the headland's height.
It shall be for remembrance   among my people
As it towers high   on the Cape of the Whale,
And sailors shall know it   as Beowulf's Barrow,
Sea-faring mariners   driving their ships
Through fogs of ocean   from far countries."
   Then the great-hearted king   unclasped from his throat
A collar of gold,   and gave to his thane;
Gave the young hero   his gold-decked helmet,
His ring and his byrny,   and wished him well:
"You are the last   of the Wægmunding line.
All my kinsmen,   eorls in their glory,
Fate has sent   to their final doom,
And I must follow."   These words were the last
The old king spoke   ere the pyre received him,
The leaping flames   of the funeral blaze,
And his breath went forth   from his bosom, his soul
Went forth from the flesh,   to the joys of the just.
   Then bitter it was   for Beowulf's thane
To behold his loved one   lying on earth
Suffering sore   at the end of life.
The monster that slew him,   the dreadful dragon,
Likewise lay broken   and brought to his death.
The worm no longer   could rule the hoard,

But the hard, sharp sword,   the work of the hammer,
Had laid him low;   and the winged dragon
Lay stretched near the barrow,   broken and still.
No more in the midnight   he soared in air,
Disclosing his presence,   and proud of his gold;
For he sank to earth   by the sword of the king.

But few of mankind,   if the tales be true,
Has it prospered much,   though mighty in war
And daring in deed,   to encounter the breath
Of the venomous worm   or plunder his wealth
When the ward of the barrow   held watch o'er the mound.
Beowulf bartered   his life for the treasure;
Both foes had finished   this fleeting life.

Not long was it then   till the laggards in battle
Came forth from the forest,   ten craven in fight,
Who had dared not face   the attack of the foe
In their lord's great need.   The shirkers in shame
Came wearing their bucklers   and trappings of war
Where the old man lay.   They looked upon Wiglaf.
Weary he sat   by the side of his leader
Attempting with water   to waken his lord.
It availed him little;   the wish was vain!
He could not stay   his soul upon earth,
Nor one whit alter   the will of God.
The Lord ruled over   the lives of men
As He rules them still.   With a stern rebuke
He reproached the cowards   whose courage had failed.
Wiglaf addressed them;   Weohstan's son
Gazed sad of heart   on the hateful men:

"Lo! he may say   who would speak the truth
That the lord who gave you   these goodly rings,
This warlike armor   wherein you stand—
When oft on the ale-bench   he dealt to his hall-men
Helmet and byrny,   endowing his thanes
With the fairest he found   from near or from far—
That he grievously wasted   these trappings of war
When battle befell him.   The king of the folk

Had no need to boast   of his friends in the fight.
But the God of victory   granted him strength
To avenge himself   with the edge of the sword
When he needed valor.   Of little avail
The help I brought   in the bitter battle!
Yet still I strove,   though beyond my strength,
To aid my kinsman.   And ever the weaker
The savage foe   when I struck with my sword;
Ever the weaker   the welling flame!
Too few defenders   surrounded our ruler
When the hour of evil   and terror befell.
Now granting of treasure   and giving of swords,
Inherited land-right   and joy of the home,
Shall cease from your kindred.   And each of your clan
Shall fail of his birthright   when men from afar
Hear tell of your flight   and your dastardly deed.
Death is better   for every eorl
Than life besmirched   with the brand of shame!"...

The Funeral Pyre *

Then the son of Weohstan,   stalwart in war,
Bade send command   to the heads of homes
To bring from afar   the wood for the burning
Where the good king lay: "Now glede shall devour,
As dark flame waxes,   the warrior prince
Who has often withstood   the shower of steel
When the storm of arrows,   sped from the string,
Broke over shield,   and shaft did service,
With feather-fittings   guiding the barb."
 Then the wise son of Weohstan   chose from the host
Seven thanes of the king,   the best of the band;
Eight heroes together   they hied to the barrow
In under the roof   of the fearful foe;
One of the warriors   leading the way
Bore in his hand   a burning brand.
They cast no lots   who should loot the treasure
When they saw unguarded   the gold in the hall
Lying there useless;   little they scrupled
As quickly they plundered   the precious store.
Over the sea-cliff   into the ocean
They tumbled the dragon,   the deadly worm,
Let the sea-tide swallow   the guarder of gold.
Then a wagon was loaded   with well-wrought treasure,
A countless number   of every kind;
And the aged warrior,   the white-haired king,
Was borne on high   to the Cape of the Whale.
 The Geat folk fashioned   a peerless pyre
Hung round with helmets   and battle-boards,
With gleaming byrnies   as Beowulf bade.
In sorrow of soul   they laid on the pyre
Their mighty leader,   their well-loved lord.
The warriors kindled   the bale on the barrow,

* *Beowulf* 3110–82.

Wakened the greatest   of funeral fires.
Dark o'er the blaze   the wood-smoke mounted;
The winds were still,   and the sound of weeping
Rose with the roar   of the surging flame
Till the heat of the fire   had broken the body.
With hearts that were heavy   they chanted their sorrow,
Singing a dirge   for the death of their lord;
And an aged woman   with upbound locks
Lamented for Beowulf,   wailing in woe.
Over and over   she uttered her dread
Of sorrow to come,   of bloodshed and slaughter,
Terror of battle,   and bondage and shame.
The smoke of the bale-fire   rose to the sky!

    The men of the Weder folk   fashioned a mound
Broad and high   on the brow of the cliff,
Seen from afar   by seafaring men.
Ten days they worked   on the warrior's barrow
Inclosing the ash   of the funeral flame
With a wall as worthy   as wisdom could shape.
They bore to the barrow   the rings and the gems,
The wealth of the hoard   the heroes had plundered.
The olden treasure   they gave to the earth,
The gold to the ground,   where it still remains
As useless to men   as it was of yore.

    Then round the mound   rode the brave in battle,
The sons of warriors,   twelve in a band,
Bemoaning their sorrow   and mourning their king.
They sang their dirge   and spoke of the hero
Vaunting his valor   and venturous deeds.
So is it proper   a man should praise
His friendly lord   with a loving heart,
When his soul must forth   from the fleeting flesh.
So the folk of the Geats,   the friends of his hearth,
Bemoaned the fall   of their mighty lord;
Said he was kindest   of worldly kings,
Mildest, most gentle,   most eager for fame.

VI

RELIGIOUS ALLEGORY

RELIGIOUS ALLEGORY

The medieval Church, to add emphasis and vividness to religious instruction, not infrequently employed allegory, and we find its shaping spirit in many Old English Christian poems. This is true of *The Whale* and *The Phoenix* of the Exeter Book. *The Whale* comprises lines 75-162 of the Old English *Physiologus*. *The Phoenix* is a complete and separate poem of 677 lines.

The legend of the Great Whale is undoubtedly of very early date. The sea-beast resembling an island, on which sailors landed and kindled a fire only to be carried down into the depths of ocean, was described in the Greek *Physiologus* as a huge sea-turtle. But in the Old English poem it is called a whale, and the description is unmistakable. In the allegorical equations of the Old English version the whale is Satan. The enticing odor that comes from the mouth of the whale is the lust of the flesh. The great jaws that close on unwary schools of fish are the gates of hell closing on the damned. The error of the sailors who mistake evil for good, and danger for safety, is the tragic error that leads to hell.

A more skillful and artistic use of allegory in Old English verse is found in *The Phoenix*, a poem which is much more than an allegorical fable. It is fashioned from a Latin poem usually attributed to Lactantius, and is one of the most graceful of the Old English religious poems. It has been claimed by some critics as the work of Cynewulf, but there is little to throw light on its authorship. The most definite conviction that comes from a study of *The Phoenix* is that its unknown author was one of the most gifted of the Old English religious poets.

The landscape of *The Phoenix* is the landscape of the Earthly Paradise. It is a tableland whose fertile soil is watered by sweet fountains, where in serene, unchanging weather no leaf withers nor fruits decay, and where nothing noisome ever intrudes. It lies near the Heavenly Paradise through whose open portals can be heard the hymns of the blessed.

At the end of every thousand years the Phoenix flies to a remote region of Syria, where in a lofty tree it builds its nest of spice-bearing twigs and fragrant herbs. There it lodges until by the sun's heat the nest kindles, and the bird is consumed. But from the ashes the Phoenix is reborn. The allegory is clearly interpreted in the poem itself. The flight of the bird from the Earthly Paradise is man's loss of Eden. The high tree in Syria is God's mercy to men. The spices and herbs of which the nest is built are the words and deeds of righteousness. In the final lines of the poem the Phoenix is explicitly equated with Christ and the Resurrection.

The Whale *

Now I will fashion   the tale of a fish,
With wise wit singing   in measured strains
The song of the Great Whale.   Often unwittingly
Ocean-mariners   meet with this monster,
Fastitocalon,   fierce and menacing,
The Great Sea-Swimmer   of the ocean-streams.
   Like a rough rock   is the Whale's appearance,
Or as if there were swaying   by the shore of the sea
A great mass of sedge   in the midst of the sand dunes;
So it seems to sailors   they see an island,
And they firmly fasten   their high-prowed ships
With anchor-ropes   to the land that is no land,
Hobble their sea-steeds   at ocean's end,
Land bold on the island   and leave their barks
Moored at the water's edge   in the wave's embrace.
   There they encamp,   the sea-weary sailors,
Fearing no danger.   They kindle a fire;
High on the island   the hot flames blaze
And joy returns   to travel-worn hearts
Eager for rest.   Then, crafty in evil,
When the Whale feels the sailors   are fully set
And firmly lodged,   enjoying fair weather,
Suddenly with his prey   Ocean's Guest plunges
Down in the salt wave   seeking the depths,
In the hall of death   drowning sailors and ships.
   Such is the manner of demons,   the devils' way,
Luring from virtue,   inciting to lust,
By secret power   deceiving men's souls
That they may seek help   at the hands of their foes
And, fixed in sin,   find abode with the Fiend.
Sly and deceitful,   when the Devil perceives

---

* *Physiologus* 75–162.

Out of hell-torment   that each of mankind,
Of the race of men,   is bound with his ring,
Then with cunning craft   the Dark Destroyer
Takes proud and humble   who here on earth
Through sin did his will.   Seizing them suddenly
Shrouded in darkness,   estranged from good,
He seeks out hell,   the bottomless abyss
In the misty gloom;   even as the Great Whale
Who drowns the mariners,   sea-steeds and men.

A second trait has he,   the proud Sea-Thrasher,
Even more marvelous: when hunger torments
And the fierce Water-Monster   is fain of food,
Then the Ocean-Warden   opens his mouth,
Unlocks his wide jaws,   and a winsome odor
Comes from his belly;   other kinds of fish
Are deceived thereby,   all eagerly swimming
To where the sweet fragrance   comes flowing forth.
In unwary schools   they enter within
Till the wide mouth is filled. Then swiftly the Whale
Over his sea-prey   snaps his grim jaws.

So is it with him   in this transient time
Who takes heed to his life   too late and too little,
Letting vain delights   through their luring fragrance
Ensnare his soul   till he slips away,
Soiled with sin,   from the King of glory.
Before them the Devil   after death's journey
Throws open hell   for all who in folly
Fulfilled the lying   lusts of the flesh
Against the law.   But when the Wily One,
Expert in evil,   has brought into bonds
In the burning heat   those cleaving to him
Laden with sins,   who during their life-days
Did his bidding,   on them after death
His savage jaws   he snaps together,
The gates of hell.   Who gather there
Know no retreat,   no return out thence,

Any more than the fishes   swimming the sea
Can escape from the grip   of the Great Whale.
   Therefore by every means   (should every man
Serve the Lord God)   and strive against devils
By words and works,   that we may behold
The King of glory.   In this transient time
Let us seek for peace   and healing at His hands,
That we in grace may dwell   with Him so dear
And have His bliss   and blessedness for ever!

The Phoenix *

Lo! I have learned   of the loveliest of lands
Far to the eastward,   famous among men.
But few ever fare   to that far-off realm
Set apart from the sinful   by the power of God.
Beauteous that country   and blessed with joys,
With the fairest odors   of all the earth;
Goodly the island,   gracious the Maker,
Matchless and mighty,   who stablished the world.
There ever stand open   the portals of heaven
With songs of rapture   for blessed souls.
  The plain is winsome,   the woods are green,
Widespread under heaven.   No rain or snow,
Or breath of frost   or blast of fire,
Or freezing hail   or fall of rime,
Or blaze of sun   or bitter-long cold,
Or scorching summer   or winter storm
Work harm a whit,   but the plain endures
Sound and unscathed.   The lovely land
Is rich with blossoms.   No mountains rise,
No lofty hills,   as here with us;
No high rock-cliffs,   no dales or hollows,
No mountain gorges,   no caves or crags,
Naught rough or rugged;   but the pleasant plain
Basks under heaven   laden with bloom.
  Twelve cubits higher   is that lovely land,
As learned writers   in their books relate,
Than any of these hills   that here in splendor
Tower on high   under heavenly stars.
Serene that country   sunny groves gleaming;
Winsome the woodlands;   fruits never fail
Or shining blossoms.   As God gave bidding
The groves stand for ever   growing and green.

* *The Phoenix* 1–392.

Winter and summer   the woods alike
Are hung with blossoms;   under heaven no leaf
Withers, no fire   shall waste the plain
To the end of the world.   As the waters of old,
The sea-floods, covered   the compass of earth
And the pleasant plain   stood all uninjured,
By the grace of God   unhurt and unharmed,
So shall it flourish   till the fire of Judgment
When graves shall open,   the dwellings of death.
   Naught hostile lodges   in all that land,
No pain or weeping   or sign of sorrow,
No age or anguish   or narrow death;
No ending of life   or coming of evil,
No feud or vengeance   or fret of care;
No lack of wealth   or pressure of want,
No sorrow or sleeping   or sore disease.
No winter storm   or change of weather
Fierce under heaven,   or bitter frost
With wintry icicles   smites any man there.
No hail or hoar-frost   descends to earth,
No windy cloud;   no water falls
Driven by storm.   But running streams
And welling waters   wondrously spring
Overflowing earth   from fountains fair.
   From the midst of the wood   a winsome water
Each month breaks out   from the turf of earth,
Cold as the sea-stream,   coursing sweetly
Through all the grove.   By the bidding of God
The flood streams forth   through the glorious land
Twelve times yearly.   The trees are hung
With beauteous increase,   flowering buds;
Holy under heaven   the woodland treasures
Wane not nor wither;   no failing bloom,
No fruits of the wildwood,   fall to earth;
But in every season   on all the trees
The boughs bear their burden   of fruit anew.
Green are the groves   in the grassy meadow,

Gaily garnished   by the might of God.
No branch is broken,   and fragrance fair
Fills all the land.   Nor ever comes change
Till the Ruler Whose wisdom   wrought its beginning
His ancient Creation   shall bring to its end.

In that woodland dwelleth,   most wondrous fair
And strong of wing,   a fowl called Phoenix;
There dauntless-hearted   he has his home,
His lonely lodging.   In that lovely land
Death shall never   do him a hurt,
Or work him harm   while the world standeth.

Each day he observes   the sun's bright journey
Greeting God's candle,   the gleaming gem,
Eagerly watching   till over the ocean
The fairest of orbs   shines forth from the East,
God's bright token   glowing in splendor,
The ancient hand-work   of the Father of all.
The stars are hid   in the western wave,
Dimmed at dawn,   and the dusky night
Steals darkly away;   then, strong of wing
And proud of pinion,   the bird looks out
Over the ocean   under the sky,
Eagerly waiting   when up from the East
Heaven's gleam comes gliding   over the wide water.

Then the fair bird,   changeless in beauty,
Frequents at the fountain   the welling streams;
Twelve times the blessed one   bathes in the burn
Ere the bright beacon comes,   the candle of heaven;
And even as often   at every bath
Tastes the pleasant water   of brimcold wells.

Thereafter the proud one   after his water-play
Takes his flight   to a lofty tree
Whence most easily   o'er the eastern ways
He beholds the course   of the heavenly taper
Brightly shining   over the tossing sea,
A blaze of light.   The land is made beautiful,
The world made fair,   when the famous gem

O'er the ocean-stretches   illumines the earth
All the world over,   noblest of orbs.
  When the sun climbs high   over the salt streams
The gray bird wings   from his woodland tree
And, swift of pinion,   soars to the sky
Singing and caroling   to meet the sun.
Then is the bearing   of the bird so fair,
Its heart so gladsome   and so graced with joy,
It trills its song   in clear-voiced strain,
More wondrous music   than ever child of man
Heard under heaven   since the High-King,
Author of glory,   created the world,
The earth and the heavens.   The music of its hymn
Is sweeter than all song-craft,   more winsome and fair
Than any harmony.   Neither trumpet nor horn,
Nor melody of harp   is like to that lay,
Nor voice of man,   nor strain of organ music,
Nor swan's singing feathers,   nor any pleasant sound
That God gave for joy to men   in this mournful world.
  So he hymns and carols   with joyous heart
Until the sun   in the southern sky
Sinks to its setting.   Then in silence he listens;
Thrice the wise-hearted   lifts his head,
Thrice shakes his feathers   strong in flight,
Then broods in silence.   Twelve times the bird
Notes the hours   of night and day.
  So is it ordained   for the forest dweller
To live in that land   having joy of life,
Well-being and bliss   and all the world's beauty,
Till the warden of the wood   of this life's winters
Has numbered a thousand.   Aged and old
The gray-plumed is weary   and weighted with years.
  Then the fairest of fowls   flies from the greenwood,
The blossoming earth,   seeks a boundless realm,
A land and lodging   where no man dwells;
And there exalted   over all the host
Has dominion and rule   of the race of birds,

With them in the waste   resides for a season.
Swift of pinion   and strong in flight
He wings to the westward,   heavy with years.
Around the royal one   throng the birds,
Servants and thanes   of a peerless prince.
And so he seeks out   the Syrian land
With a lordly following.   There the pure fowl
Suddenly leaves them,   lodging in shadow
In a woodland covert,   a secret spot
Sequestered and hidden   from the hosts of men.

   There he takes lodging   in a lofty tree
Fast by its roots   in the forest-wood
Under heaven's roof.   The race of men
Call the tree Phoenix   from the name of the fowl.
Unto that tree,   as I have heard tell,
The Great King has granted,   the Lord of mankind,
That it alone   of all tall trees
Is the brightest blooming   in all the earth.
Nor may aught of evil   work it a harm;
For ever shielded,   for ever unscathed,
It stands to the end   while the world standeth.

   When the wind lies at rest   and weather is fair,
And heaven's bright gem   shines holy on high,
When clouds are dispersed   and seas are tranquil
And every storm   is stilled under heaven,
When the weather-candle   shines warm from the south
Lighting earth's legions,   then in the boughs
He begins to form   and fashion a nest.
His sage heart stirs   with a great desire
Swiftly to alter   old age to youth,
To renew his life.   From near and far
He gleans and gathers   to his lodging-place
Pleasant plants   and fruits of the forest,
All sweetest spices   and fragrant herbs
Which the King of glory,   Lord of beginnings,
Created on earth   for a blessing to men,
The sweetest under heaven.   So he assembles

In the boughs of the tree   his shining treasures.
There in that waste-land   the wild bird
In the tall tree's top   timbers his house
Pleasant and lovely.   And there he lodges
In that lofty chamber;   in the leafy shade
Besets his feathered body   on every side
With the sweetest odors   and blossoms of earth.
   When the gem of the sky   in the summer season,
The burning sun,   shines over the shades
Scanning the world,   the Phoenix sits
Fain of departure,   fulfilling his fate.
His house is kindled   by heat of the sun;
The herbs grow hot,   the pleasant hall steams
With sweetest odors;   in the surging flame,
In the fire-grip, burns   the bird with his nest.
The pyre is kindled,   the fire enfolds
The home of the heart-sick.   The yellow flame
Fiercely rages;   the Phoenix burns,
Full of years,   as the fire consumes
The fleeting body.   The spirit fades,
The soul of the fated.   The bale-fire seizes
Both bone and flesh.
                        But his life is reborn
After a season,   when the ashes begin
After the fire-surge   fusing together
Compressed to a ball.   The brightest of nests,
The house of the stout-heart,   by force of the flame
Is clean consumed;   the corpse grows chill;
The bone-frame is broken;   the burning subsides.
From the flame of the fire   is found thereafter
In the ash of the pyre   an apple's likeness,
Of which grows a worm   most wondrous fair,
As it were a creature   come from an egg,
Shining from the shell.   In the shadow it grows
Fashioned first   as an eagle's young,
A comely fledgling;   then flourishing fair
Is like in form   to a full-grown eagle

Adorned with feathers   as he was at first,
Brightly gleaming.
                    Then is beauty reborn,
Sundered from sin,   once more made new;
Even in such fashion   as men, for food,
Bring home in harvest   at reaping time
Pleasant fare,   the fruits of earth,
Ere coming of winter   lest rain-storms waste;
Find joy and strength   in their garnered store
When frost and snow   with furious might
Cover earth over   with winter weeds:
From these grains again   grow riches for men
Through the sprouting kernels,   first sowed pure seed;
Then the warm sun in Spring-time,   symbol of life,
Wakes the world's wealth   and new crops rise,
Each after its kind,   the treasures of earth.

   Even so the Phoenix   after long life
Grows young and fashioned   with flesh anew.
He eats no food,   no fare of earth,
But only a drop   of honey-dew
Which falls in the midnight;   thereby the Phoenix
Comforts his life   till he comes again
To his own habitation,   his ancient seat.

   Beset with his sweet herbs,   proud of plumage,
The bird is reborn,   his life made young,
Youthful and gifted   with every grace.
Then from the ground   he gathers together
The nimble body   that the bale-fire broke;
With skill assembles   the ashy remnants,
The crumbling bones   left after the blaze;
Brings together there   bone and ashes
And covers over   with savory herbs
The spoil of the death-fire,   fairly adorned.

   Then he takes his departure,   turns to his home,
Grasps in his talons,   clasps in his claws,
What the fire has left;   joyously flying
To his native dwelling,   his sun-bright seat,

His happy homeland.   All is renewed,
Life and feathered body   as it was at first
What time God placed him   in that pleasant plain.
He brings there the bones   which the fiery surges
Swallowed in flame   on the funeral pyre,
The ashes as well;   and all together
Buries the leavings,   ashes and bone,
In his island home.   For him is renewed
The sign of the sun   when the light of heaven,
Brightest of orbs,   most joyous of jewels,
Over the ocean   shines from the East.
   Fair-breasted that fowl   and comely of hue
With varied colors;   the head behind
Is emerald burnished   and blended with scarlet.
The tail plumes are colored   some crimson, some brown,
And cunningly speckled   with shining spots.
White of hue   are the backs of the wings,
The neck all green   beneath and above.
The strong neb gleams   like glass or gem;
Without and within   the beak is fair.
The eye is stark,   most like to stone
Or shining jewel   skillfully wrought
In a golden setting   by cunning smiths.
All round the neck   like the ring of the sun
Is a shining circlet   fashioned of feathers.
Wondrously bright   and shining the belly,
Brilliant and comely;   over the back
Splendidly fashioned   the shield is spread.
The fair bird's shanks,   its yellow feet
Are patterned with scales.   'Tis a peerless fowl
Most like in appearance   to a peacock proud,
As the writings say;   neither sluggish or slow,
Torpid or slothful,   as some birds are
Heavily winging   their way in the sky;
But swift and lively   and very light,
Fair and goodly   and marked with glory.
Eternal the God   who grants him that grace!

Then from that country   the Phoenix flies
To seek his homeland,   his ancient seat.
He wings his way   observed of men
Assembled together   from south and north,
From East and west,   in hurrying hosts.
A great folk gathers   from far and near
To behold God's grace   in the beauteous bird
For whom at Creation   the Lord of all
Ordained and stablished   a special nature,
A fairer perfection   beyond all fowl.
Men on earth   all marvel in wonder
At the fair fowl's beauty   inscribing in books
And skillfully carving   on marble stone
When the day and the hour   shall exhibit to men
The gleaming beauty   of the flying bird.

Then all about him   the race of birds
In flocks assemble   on every side,
Winging from far ways,   singing his praises,
Hymning their hero   in fervent strains;
Around the Phoenix   in circling flight
They attend the holy one   high in air,
Thronging in multitudes.   Men look up,
Marvel to see   that happy host
Worship the wild bird,   flock after flock,
Keenly acclaiming   and praising as King
Their beloved lord;   joyously leading
Their liege to his home;   till at last alone
He swiftly soars   where that blissful band
May not follow after   when the best of birds
From the turf of earth   returns to his homeland.

So the blessed bird   after his death-bale
Enters once more   his ancient abode,
His fatherland fair.   Leaving their leader
The birds sad-hearted   return to their home,
Their prince to his palace.   God only knows,
The Almighty King,   what his breed may be,
Or male or female;   and no man knows,

VII

OLD TESTAMENT
AND APOCRYPHAL VERSE

OLD TESTAMENT AND APOCRYPHAL VERSE

The poetic narrative of Lucifer's rebellion and the Fall of Man is found in the Old English *Genesis*, the first poem of the Junius MS. *Genesis* consists of two parts: section *A*, lines 1-234 and 852 to the end; and section *B*, lines 235-851. Section *B* is an interpolation into a break in section *A* and is, in part at least, a transcription from an Old Saxon poem. The opening lines of *Genesis* deal with the rebellion of Lucifer, and this material is supplemented in *Christ and Satan*, of the same MS, by a series of "lamentations" of the fallen angels. After rehearsing the rebellion and fall of Lucifer, *Genesis* goes on to recount the story of Creation and the Fall of Man.

In *Genesis B* and *Christ and Satan*, both source material and its poetic shaping go far beyond Biblical paraphrase. In both poems we find dramatic versification of material gathered from many sources and blended into what became known as the Hexaemeral tradition. The stream of this tradition included commentaries on the Hexaemeron, or six days of the Creation as recorded in the Biblical Genesis, and the exegetical writings of the Church Fathers.

A series of Lenten sermons by Bishop Basil of Caesarea was an early work specifically devoted to discussion of the Creation. Against a Scriptural background, there came to be associated with the story of Creation accounts of the Revolt of the Angels and the Fall of Man. The inclusion of these three themes in poetic form in the Junius MS takes on the nature of an unformed cosmic trilogy. In the volume and scope of the Hexaemeral tradition we find apocryphal legend like the *Vita* of Adam and Eve; patristic commentary such as Bede's *Commentary on Genesis*, an Old English *Hexaemeron* often attributed to Ælfric; and similar writings of Churchmen and scholars.

The temptation scene in *Genesis B* varies in important respects from the Biblical account. The Tempter appears to Adam and Eve disguised as an angelic messenger claiming that God has sent him to revoke the ban on the forbidden fruit. Rejected by Adam he turns to Eve, who is convinced and eats of the fruit. She joins in persuading Adam to eat, saying she knows by the messenger's raiment that he comes from God, and that Adam is refusing obedience to God's new command. All this she does, the poet tells us, with a loyal heart. The assumption of angelic form by agents of evil is, of course, not unique in *Genesis B*. It is a device of deception employed in the apocryphal *Vita* of Adam and Eve, and found in many legends of the saints, among them Cynewulf's poem based on a Latin life of St. Juliana of Nicomedia.

Lamentations of the Fallen Angels *

There out of hell   the Old One bellows
With bitter outcry   and baleful voice
Bewailing his woe: "Whither is fled
The wealth of bliss   we should have in heaven?
This is the home of darkness   dreadfully bound
With fettering bonds of fire.   The floor of hell
Is a blaze of flame   burning with poison.
Not far is the end   when we all together
Must suffer torment,   torture and pain,
No longer possessing   the splendor of glory
In heaven above,   or joy in her high halls.

   "Lo!   once of old   before the face of God
In happier hours   we knew heavenly bliss
Singing in glory,   where now round Eternal God
The righteous dwell   in heaven's high hall
Adoring the Lord   with words and works,
While I in this torment   must abide in bonds,
Nor hope for a better home,   because of my pride. . . .

   "I was a holy angel   in heaven of old
Dear unto God;   knew delight with the Lord,
Great joy with our Maker;   this multitude likewise.
But I planned in my heart   to hurl from His throne
The Splendor of glory,   the Son of God;
To rule over all things   with this wretched band
Which I have brought home to hell.   Clear was the token
When I was cast down to perdition,   deep under earth
To the bottomless pit.   I have brought you all
From your native home   to a house of bondage.

   "Here is no glory of wealth,   no wine-hall of the proud,
No worldly joys or angelic,   no hope of heaven.
This foul home flames with fire.   I am God's foe!
Ever at the doors of hell   dragons stand guard

* *Christ and Satan* 34–50; 81–105; 129–77.

Fierce and flaming.   Hope not for help from them!
This terrible home   is filled full with horror.
We have nowhere to hide our heads   in the gloom of hell,
Or cover ourselves in the depths   with shadows of darkness.
Here is the adder's hiss!   Here serpents dwell!
Firmly the bonds of pain   are fastened upon us.
Fierce are the fiends of hell,   dusky and dark.
Day never lightens this gloom   nor the glory of God. . . .
    "I am so large of limb   I may not lie hid
In this wide hall,   wounded with my sins.
At times cold and heat   in hell are mingled;
At times I can hear   the hell-slaves howl,
A wretched race   bewailing this realm of pain
Deep under the nesses   where naked men
Struggle with serpents.   All this windy hall
Is filled with horror.   Never shall I know
A happier home,   city or stronghold,
Nor ever mine eyes have sight   of the gleaming world again.
    "Worse is it now for me   that ever I knew
The gleaming light of glory   with angels on high,
And the harmonies of heaven   where hosts of the blessed
Encircle the Son of God   with sweetest song.
No evil can I bring   on any soul
Except those only   whom God casts out.
These I may have in thrall   in the bondage of hell,
Bring to their long abode   in the bitter abyss.
    "How unlike are we all   to those earlier days
When once we had beauty in heaven,   honor and bliss.
Often the sons of God   sang hymns of glory
When as thanes about our Beloved   we praised the Lord,
Sang glory to God.   But now I am stained with my sins,
Branded with evil;   now burning with fire
I must bear on my back   the bondage of torment,
Hot in hell,   without hope of good."
    And still the Foul Fiend,   shepherd of sins,
Cried out of hell   in torment accursed.
The words he spoke   flew forth in sparks,

Most like to poison   as he poured them out:
　"Farewell to the glory of God!　Farewell to the Helm of hosts!
Farewell to the might of the Maker.　Farewell to the world!
Farewell to the light of day　and the grace of God!
Farewell to the angel host!　Farewell to heaven!
Alas! that I have lost　those lasting joys!
Alas! that I may not reach with my hands　to heaven above,
Nor thither lift up mine eyes,　nor hear with my ears
The pealing trumpet sound,　because from His seat
I would have driven God's Son　and seized for myself
Dominion of glory and grace.　Worse fate befell
Than I could foresee.　From the shining host I am severed,
Cast down from light　into this loathsome home."

The Temptation and Fall of Man *

With mighty hand   the Holy Lord,
All-Ruling God,   had stablished and strengthened
Ten angel orders   in whom He trusted
That they would serve Him   and work His will,
Since the Holy Lord   with His hands had shaped them,
Had given them reason   and granted them bliss.
    He made one so strong,   so mighty of mind;
Gave him such power   next unto God
In the heavenly kingdom;   shaped him so shining;
So fair the form   God fashioned for him;
That his beauty was like   to the blazing stars.
He should have said praises   and prayers unto God,
Prizing his bliss   and blessing in heaven;
Should have thanked his Lord   for His gifts in light
Which God would have let him   long enjoy.
But he turned it all   to a terrible outcome;
Began to stir up   strife against God,
Heaven's Highest Ruler   on His holy throne. . . .
    "Why must I slave?   What need (quoth he)
That I serve a master?   My hands have might
To work many wonders.   I have strength to rear
A goodlier throne,   a higher in heaven.
Why must I yield   or fawn for His favor
Or bow in submission?   I may be God
As well as He.   Brave comrades stand by me,
Stout-hearted heroes   unfailing in strife.
These fighters fierce   have made me their leader;
With such may one plan   and muster support.
They are loyal friends   and faithful of heart;
I may be their lord   and rule this realm.
So it seems not good   that I grovel before God
For any boon.   I will obey Him no longer."

* *Genesis* 246–60; 278–300; 347–88; 408–730; 751–62.

Now when the Almighty   had heard these words,
How the arrogant angel   was rousing revolt
From his Lord and Leader   in insolent folly,
Needs must he pay   for that deed of pride,
Know the pain of that struggle,   and suffer his punishment,
Most dreadful of deaths.   So every man shall,
Whoever wickedly   wars against God,
The Lord of might!   Heaven's Ruler was roused
And hurled him in wrath   from his heavenly throne. . . .
   Then spoke Satan   in sorrow of spirit,
Who must henceforth rule   o'er the depths of hell.
Once he was white,   God's angel in heaven,
Till his heart betrayed him,   his haughty pride,
And he would not obey   or honor the word
Of the Lord of hosts.   Hell's heat was around him,
His heart surged within him;   he spoke these words:
   "Unlike indeed   is this narrow land
To that other home   that of old we held
In heaven's high realm,   though we could not keep
What our Lord had granted,   or govern our kingdom
Against God's will.   He has wrought us wrong,
In hurling us down   to the fiery depths of hell,
Deprived of heaven.   He has marked those heights
For man to settle. 'Tis my greatest sorrow
That Adam, fashioned   and formed of earth,
Should hold my high seat   and abide in bliss
While we suffer this torture,   this torment in hell.
   "Woe! Alas!   Could I lift my hands
And feel their strength,   be free for an hour,
One winter hour,   with this host I would—
But bands of iron   bind me about,
Sorely the rings   of my bondage ride me!
I am stripped of my kingdom.   Firmly hell's fetters
Are fastened upon me;   the fires burn
Above and below.   A loathlier landscape
I never have seen,   flame unassuaged
Surging through hell.   These clasping shackles,

These cruel-hard chains,   hinder my going.
Hell's doors are bolted,   the ways are barred,
My hands are fastened,   my feet are bound,
I can no way get free   of these fettering chains.
Gratings huge   of heavy iron,
Hammered hot,   press hard upon me,
Wherewith God has fastened me   firm by the neck.
I know full well   that He knew my purpose
Of evil for Adam   and all his hopes
Of the heavenly realm,   had I power of my hands. . . .
     "Begin now to plan   and plot this assault!
If to any thane ever   in days of old
When we dwelt in that good kingdom   and happily held our thrones
I dealt out princely treasure,   at no dearer time
Could he give me requital,   repayment for gifts,
If some thane would be my helper   and outward hence
Break through these bolted gates,   with strength to wing
On feathered pinions   circling in the sky
To where new-shaped on earth   Adam and Eve
Abide in bliss   surrounded with abundance,
While we are cast out hither   to this deep hell.
     "They now indeed   are dearer unto God
And have the wealth   that we should have in heaven,
Our rightful realm.   The advantage lies with man!
My soul is sorrowful,   my heart is sore
That they should hold   the heavenly realms for ever.
If one of you can win them   in any way
To forsake God's law,   they will lose His love;
If they break His commandment   His mood will be roused
And all their wealth   will be changed for the worse,
Their punishment made ready,   some penalty grim.
Take thought how you may ensnare them.   More softly then
Shall I lie in these chains   if they lose the heavenly kingdom.
Whoever shall bring that to pass   shall have portion for ever
In all we may win of advantage   in these wide flames.
I will let him sit next myself   who returns to tell,
In this hot hell,   that the will of the King of heaven

Unworthily they forswore   by their words and works.". . .[1]
   Then God's enemy   began to arm,
To put on his war-gear.   He had a wily heart.
He placed on his head   the helmet of darkness,
Fastened the buckles   and bound it firm.
He had craft of speech   and cunning of word.
He circled upward   and darted out
Through the portals of hell.   (He had a pitiless heart.)
Fell of purpose   he soared in flight
Cleaving the fire   with fiendish craft.
He wished to ensnare   God's servants in sin,
Seduce and beguile them   until they had gained God's hate.
   With fiendish cunning   he found his way
To where on earth   he came upon Adam,
God's own handiwork   wisely fashioned
And Eve beside him,   fairest of women,
Serving God well   in all good works
For the Maker of man   had made them His stewards.
   By them two trees stood   filled with fruit
And clothed with increase.   Heaven's High King,
The Almighty, had set them   that the sons of men
Might choose of good or evil,   weal or woe.
   Unlike was their fruit.   One tree was fair,
Lovely and shining,   pleasant and sweet.
That was the tree of life!   He might live for ever,
Who ate of that fruit.   Nor would age thereafter
Or woeful sickness   work him a hurt;
But long might he live   in happiness for ever,
Have here on earth   the favor of heaven's King
And the glory ordained on high   when he went hence.
   The other tree was in shadow,   sunless and dark;
That was the tree of death!   Deadly its fruit!

---

[1] At this point in the MS a leaf or two is missing. The lost text
must have dealt in some detail with the response to this *comitatus*
appeal of the chained and shackled Satan. Evidently one of his
followers came forward and was accepted as his agent in evil. As
the text continues after the break, this deputy of Satan is pictured
as "God's enemy" arming himself for the work of revenge.

Disgraced in this world,   knowing good and evil,
He needs must suffer   in sorrow and sweat
Who ate of the fruit   that formed on that tree.
Old age would despoil him   of deeds of strength,
Of bliss and lordship,   with death for his lot.
A little time only   he might joy in this life,
Then seek in the flames   the most loathsome of lands,
Be subject to fiends   where most fearful horrors
Afflict men for ever.   That the fiend knew well,
The devil's dark steward   who strove against God.

   Then the fiend put on   the form of the serpent
In twining coils   round the tree of death;
Took of the fruit   and turned him thence
To where he saw Adam,   God's handiwork.
With wily falsehood   from the first word
The devil began   to ask of Adam:

   "Have you any longing, Adam,   that looks to God?
I come in His service,   faring from afar;
Nor has time been long   since I sat at His side.
On this errand He sent me,   bade you eat of this fruit;
Said your power and might   and your mind will be greater,
Your body brighter,   your form more fair,
And you shall lack naught   of the world's wealth.
Because you have done His will   and won His favor,
And served Him with gladness,   you are dear unto God.
In His heavenly light   I have heard Him speak
Of your way of life,   praising your words and works.

   "So must you also   obey the bidding
His heralds bring you   hither to this land.
Wide reaching   are the green realms of the world
And God, the All-Ruler,   reigns in the highest heavens.
He does not wish   to have the hardship
Of making this journey   but sends His servants
To tell His commandments,   bidding us teach
Wisdom by precept.   Now do His will,
Take this fruit in your hand,   taste it and eat.
Your heart will grow roomy,   your form more fair.

The Lord, your God,   sent this help from heaven."
    Then Adam answered   where he stood on earth,
The first of men: "When I heard the Almighty,
The Victor Lord speaking   with solemn voice,
And He bade me dwell here   and do His will,
Gave me the woman,   this glowing bride,
And bade me guard   that I be not beguiled
Or ever tempted   to the tree of death,
He said that blackest hell   shall hold him fast
Who harbors in his heart   one whit of evil.
Though you come with lies   and with cunning guile
I do not know   that you come from God,
An angel from heaven.   I can understand nothing
Of the bidding you bring,   of your errand or sayings,
Of your words or ways.   But well I know
What our Saviour said   when last I saw Him:
To honor His word   and keep it well,
To fulfill His law.   You are not like
Any of His angels   that ever I saw,
Nor do I find in you   any token of faith
That God has sent me   as sign of His favor.
Therefore I can not hearken.   Get you hence!
I fix my faith   on Almighty God
Whose hands created me.   From His high kingdom
He can give us all good things,   though He send no servant."
    Then the tempter in anger   turned unto Eve
Where he saw her standing,   the lovely woman.
He said that thereafter   her offspring would suffer
The worst of all evils: "I know well that God
Will be much displeased   with the message I bring,
When I come from my weary journey   over this long way
To tell Him you will not heed   the new behest
He sends you out of the East.   He only, forsooth,
Must come to instruct you;   His messengers may not
Tell you His bidding!   Truly I know
The Almighty's wrath   will be roused against you.
    "But if willingly, O woman,   you hear my words

Your mind will be freer,   your wit more firm
To ponder good counsel.   Plan in your heart
That you both may avert   the vengeance to come,
As I shall show you.   Eat of this fruit!
Then your eyes shall have light   to look afar
Over all the world,   even unto the throne
Of your Lord in heaven,   and have His favor.
Over Adam thereafter   you shall have sway
If you have the will   and he trusts your words.
If you tell him truly   the precepts you heed
To work God's will   and keep His commandments,
He will cease this strife,   these evil answers,
As we both shall urge him   to his own good.
Entreat him earnestly   to follow your teaching
Lest you grow displeasing   to the Lord, your God.
    "If you can perfect this attempt,   O fairest of women,
I will conceal from your Lord   Adam's insolent speech,
His churlish words.   He charges me with falsehood,
Says I am eager in evil,   no angel of God
But a servant of fiends!   Yet I know full well
All the angel orders   and heaven's high span,
So long was the time   I served my Lord
With loyal heart.   I am not like a devil."
    And so with lies   and with luring wiles
He urged the woman   to that deed of evil,
Till the serpent's words   began to work within her
(For God had fashioned for her   a feebler mind),
And her heart inclined   according to his counsel.
Defying God's bidding   she took from the fiend
The fatal fruit   of the tree of death.
Never was worse deed   ordained for men!
Great is the wonder   that Eternal God
Would ever permit   so many of His servants
To be tricked with lies   that came as good counsel.
    She ate of the apple   and set at naught
The word and the will   of Almighty God.
Then she saw afar   by gift of the fiend

Who misled her with lies   and shrewdly deceived her
So that earth and heaven   and all this world,
The mighty and wondrous   work of God,
Seemed to her fairer   and filled with light.
She beheld it not   by human vision
But the devil slyly   deceived her soul
And gave her sight   to see afar
O'er the heavenly kingdom.   With hostile heart
The cursed one spake: (No boon was his counsel!)
    "O worthy Eve!   You may see for yourself
How you now have altered,   nor need I tell
How bright your beauty   or your form how fair,
Since you trusted my words   and followed my teaching.
All round about you   shines radiant light
Which I brought from God,   blazing from heaven.
Lo! You may touch it!   Tell Adam in truth
What vision you have,   what virtue, through my coming.
Even yet, if humbly   he will hear my words
I will give him abundance   of this good light
Wherewith I have blessed you.   Nor will I upbraid
Or charge against him   his graceless speech
Though he does not deserve   to have it condoned,
So great the ill will   he uttered against me."
    So must their offspring   live thereafter:
When they do evil   they must earn God's grace,
Make amends to God   for their grievous wrong
And have His help   and eternal favor.
    Then went unto Adam   the fairest of women,
The winsomest maid   that ever came into this world,
For she was the handiwork   of the King of heaven,
Though so slyly ensnared   and misled with lies
That through fiendish craft   and the devil's cunning
She grew hateful to God,   forfeited His favor,
And lost her glory   and her heavenly home
For many a while.   Woe to the man
Who departs not from evil   when he has the power!
    Some she bore in her hands,   some on her breast,

Of the fatal apples,   the fruit of the tree
Which God forbade her,   the Giver of glory,
Saying His servants   need not suffer death.
Holy God gave all men   a heavenly home
And abundant blessings   if they would but forgo
The fearful harvest,   the bitter fruit,
Which that baleful tree   bore on its branches.
Those were the boughs of death   which the Lord forbade!
But the loathed of the Lord,   the tempter, betrayed her
Into God's hatred,   misled with lies;
Deceived Eve's soul,   the woman's weak will,
Till she trusted his words   and followed his teaching.
She believed that his counsel   came from God
As he cunningly said   and showed her a token,
A pledge of good faith   and of friendly heart.
Then she said to her liege:
                            "Adam, my lord,
This fruit is so sweet   and blithe in the breast;
This shining envoy   is God's good angel;
I see by his garb   he is sent by our Lord,
The Warden of heaven.   Better that we
Should win his favor   than have his ill will;
If today you made answer   with aught of evil
He will still forgive   if we do his service.
Of what avail   is this venomous strife
With the angel of God?   We need his good will.
He can plead our cause   with the Almighty Prince,
The King of heaven.   I can see from here
Where He sits in splendor   in the South and East,
Who shaped this world.   I can see His angels
Wheeling about Him   in winged flight,
Unnumbered legions,   most lovely of hosts.
Who could bestow   such virtue and vision
Unless it came   from the heavenly King?

   "Far can I hear,   far can I see
Through all the world   and the wide Creation;
I can hear the hymns   of rapture in heaven.

My heart is illumined   from without and within
Since I ate of the apple.   Here in my hands
I bring this fruit   and give of it freely.
O good my lord,   I do believe
It is come from God   and brought by His bidding,
As in truthful words   this herald has told me.
It is like naught else   in all the earth
Except, as he says,   it is sent by God."
    Over and over she urged him,   all the long day
Driving Adam   to that dark deed,
That they disobey   the bidding of God.
The fiend stood near   inflaming desire,
Boldly enticed him,   cunningly tempted.
Full close stood the fiend   who came from afar
On that fatal mission.   He planned that men
Should be driven down   unto utter death,
Deceived and misled   so that they would lose
The Almighty's gift,   the grace of God
And their heavenly home.   The hell-fiend knew
They must bear God's wrath   and bitter affliction,
Sore bondage in hell,   because they forsook
The will of God   when with lying words
He misled to that folly   the lovely maid,
The fairest of women,   till she spoke as he willed
And helped to seduce   the work of God's hand.
    Over and over   the most winsome of women
Pled with Adam   until Adam's mind
Began to change,   and he trusted the token
The woman offered.   Yet she did it all
With a loyal heart   and knew not the harm,
The fearful afflictions   that would follow for men,
When she hearkened to the counsel   of the hateful herald.
She thought by her words   to win God's favor
When she offered Adam   that token of truth
And the heart of the man   was moved in his breast,
And his soul was turned   unto Eve's desire.
    From the woman's hand   he took death and hell,

Though it bore not these names   but the name of fruit.
Yet the sleep of death   and the devil's seduction,
Death and damnation,   perdition of men,
Were the fatal fruit   whereon they had feasted.
When the apple within him   touched at his heart,
Then laughed aloud   the fierce-hearted fiend,
Capered about,   thanked his lord for both:
   "Now have I won your favor   and done your will.
For many a day   is man undone,
Adam and Eve.   They shall know God's anger
Because they neglected   His word and His will. . . .
   "Blithe may your heart be   in your breast!
For here today   are two things done:
The sons of men   shall lose their heavenly mansions
And come to your kingdom   to the fiery flames;
Also, heart-sorrow and grief   are ordained for God.
Whatsoever of evil   we suffer here
Is now repaid to Adam   in the anger of God,
In man's perdition   and the pangs of death.
Therefore my mind is healed,   my heart made roomy,
For all our harms are avenged,   and the hurt we suffered.
Now I return to the flames   and seek out Satan
Where he lies in the darkness of hell   loaded with chains."

VIII

CYNEWULF AND HIS FOLLOWERS

CYNEWULF AND HIS FOLLOWERS

With the evidence available, no poetry can be definitely attributed to Cynewulf beyond the four poems that bear his signature in runic letters, woven into the text near the end of each poem. These are the *Juliana, Elene, Ascension,* and *Fates of the Apostles.* Cynewulf's motive for his signatures was not pride of authorship or desire for fame. It was the wish of a deeply religious poet for the prayers of his readers. This he explicitly states in *Juliana,* lines 718–22: "I ask each man who may recite this poem to remember me by my name (*bi noman minum*), and pray that God may be merciful to me in the Great Day." The same motive for signature is stated in the *Fates of the Apostles.*

Of Cynewulf's signed poems two, the *Juliana* and *Elene,* are poetic narratives based on saints' legends. The legend of Juliana (*Acta Sanctorum* for February 16) tells the story of the martyrdom of St. Juliana of Nicomedia. The poem for which Cynewulf uses this material has every sign of being an early work. The *Elene* (*Acta Sanctorum* for May 4) retells in detail the Finding of the Cross by Helena, mother of the Roman Emperor Constantine. Constantine's vision of the Cross, his battle with the Huns, and Helena's embarkation and sea-voyage are vividly pictured. The *Ascension* closely parallels a Latin homily on the Ascension by Gregory. The *Fates of the Apostles* is a versified martyrology.

Other fine religious poems seem to show Cynewulfian influence, but there is no evidence as to their authorship. One of these is the *Dream of the Rood.* Set in the frame of the medieval dream-vision, it is one of the loveliest of all the Old English religious poems. It expresses with lyric grace an adoration that finds its symbol in the Cross. Because of its style, and an intimate personal reference similar to the personal passages in the signed poems, some scholars have been inclined to regard the *Dream* as the work of Cynewulf.

133

The *Advent Lyrics* are poetic elaborations of antiphons appointed to be sung in the services of the medieval Church at Lauds, Vespers, and other Hours during the Advent season. The antiphons on which they are based are variously interpretative of the significance of the Coming of Christ. The most characteristic feature of these lyrics is the blending of the poet's gift and the Churchman's concern with the doctrinal mysteries of the Advent.

The Last Judgment reflects a variety of sources. Its structural design is governed by the alphabetic hymn, *Apparebit repentina dies magna Domini*, quoted by Bede in the *De Arte Metrica*. Many passages of the poem are reflections of writings of Gregory, Augustine, Caesarius of Arles, and others. The entire poem has sustained creative energy in a cosmic panorama that begins with the sounding trumpets of Doomsday, and ends with the light of the Cross shining over all Creation, in place of the sun.

Constantine's Vision of the Cross *

The year was the sixth   of Constantine's sway
Since he was raised up   in the Roman kingdom
To be battle-lord   and leader in war.
He was eager for praise,   defender of peoples,
Unto men merciful;   his princely might
Increased under heaven.   He was true king,
War-lord of peoples.   God prospered him
In glory and might   so that for many
Through all the earth   he became a comfort,
Defending the folk,   when against the foe
He took up weapons.

                                He was threatened with war,
Tumult of battle.   The Hunnish tribe
And the Hreth-Goths also   assembled a host.
Fierce in strife   marched the Franks and the Hugas;
Bold men were they   and ready for battle.
War-spears glittered   and woven mail;
With shout and shield   they raised their standards.
The men of war   were openly mustered,
The clan was gathered,   the folk fared forth.
The wolf in the wood   sang his song of war,
Hid not his hope   of carnage to come.
The wet-winged eagle   clamored and cried
As he followed the foe.   Straight through the cities
The greatest of battle-hosts   hasted to war
In hordes as many   as the Hunnish king
Might anywhere muster   of neighboring men,
Mail-clad warriors.   The mightiest of armies
Went forth to battle   in bands made strong
With mounted legions,   till in foreign land
They boldly camped   on the Danube's bank
Near the river's torrent   with tumult of men.

* Cynewulf's *Elene* 7-147.

Fain would they conquer   the kingdom of Rome,
Plunder and waste it.   The approach of the Huns
Was known through the cities.   And Caesar bade
Against the fierce foe's   flying arrows
Summon the warriors   straightway to strife,
Bring men to battle   under the sky.
Straightway the Romans,   strong in might,
Were weaponed for battle   though their war-band was less
Than rode round the ruthless   king of the Huns.

   Then shields resounded   and war-wood sang;
The king with his troops   advanced to attack.
The raven clamored   cruel and dark.
The host moved forward;   horn-bearers leaped;
Heralds shouted;   horses trod earth;
The army assembled,   the stalwart to strife.

   Then the king was affrighted,   shaken with fear,
When he beheld   the foreign foe,
The army of Huns,   the horde of the Hreth-Goths,
Who there at the Roman   Empire's end
On the river's margin   mustered their host,
A countless force.   The Roman king
Endured heart-sorrow.   No hope had he
Of winning the battle   for want of strength.
He had too few warriors,   trusted comrades,
Against that overmight   of stalwart men.
There the army encamped,   eorls round their prince,
Near to the river   for the night-long time
After first they beheld   the march of the foe.

   Then to great Caesar   as he lay in slumber
Asleep with his train   was a vision revealed.
To him appeared   a beauteous Presence,
In man's shape   made manifest,
White and shining,   more fair of form
Than early or late   he beheld under heaven.
He started from slumber,   did on his boar-helm,
And straightway the herald,   fair heavenly form,
Spoke unto Caesar,   named him by name,

And the veil of darkness   vanished away:
   "O Constantine,   the King of angels,
Leader of nations   and Lord of fate,
Proclaims a compact.   Be not afraid
Though these foreign tribes   threaten with terror,
With hard battle.   To heaven look up,
To the Prince of glory.   There find support
And a token of triumph."
                              Straightway the king
Opened his heart   to the angel's bidding
And looked on high   as the herald bade,
Fair weaver of concord.   Clothed with treasure
O'er the roof of clouds   he beheld the Cross
Adorned with gold;   its jewels glittered.
The radiant Tree   was written round
With gleaming letters   of glowing light:
"With this sign thou shalt halt   the hostile host,
And crush the foe   in this perilous fray."
   Then the radiance faded   faring on high,
And the angel with it,   to the host of the holy.
The king was the blither,   the captain of heroes,
And the freer from sorrow   in his inmost soul
By virtue of that vision   so wondrous fair.
   Then Constantine,   the glorious king,
Protector of princes   and Giver of gifts,
War-lord of armies,   bade quickly work
And shape a symbol   like the Cross of Christ
As he saw that sign   revealed in the heavens.
He bade at dawn,   at the break of day,
Rouse the warriors   to the weapon-storm,
Lift high the standard,   the Holy Tree,
In the thick of the foe   bear the Cross before them.
   Loud o'er the legions   the trumpets sang.
The raven rejoiced;   the wet-winged eagle
Gazed on the struggle,   the cruel strife;
The wolf, woodland comrade,   lifted his wail.
Battle-terror was come.   Then was crashing of shields,

Crush of heroes   and hard hand-swing,
The slaughter of many,   when first they met
The flying darts.   Against the doomed
The stalwart fighters   with strong hand
Sent storms of arrows,   their battle-adders,
O'er the yellow shield   on the savage foe.
Stout-hearted they stormed,   fiercely attacking;
Broke through the shield-hedge;   drove home the sword.
Before the legions   the banner was lifted,
The war-song was sung.   Helmets of gold
And spear-points flashed   on the field of war.
The pagans perished;   peaceless they fell.
　　Then headlong fled   the Hunnish folk
When the Roman war-lord   waging the fight
Bade lift on high   the Holy Tree.
Heroes were scattered;   some war took;
Some barely survived   in the bitter fight;
Some half-alive   fled to a fastness,
Sheltered themselves   in the stony cliffs,
Beside the Danube   defended a stronghold;
And some at life's end drowned   in the river-depths.
　　Then the heroes exulted   pursuing the heathen
Until evening came   from the dawn of day;
Ash-spears flew,   their battle-adders.
The host was cut down,   the hated horde;
Of the Hunnish troops   but few returned home.
So was it clear   that the King Almighty
Awarded to Constantine   in that day's work
Fortune in battle,   glory and fame
And an earthly kingdom,   through the Holy Cross.

Two Rune Signatures of Cynewulf

The *Juliana* Signature*

I have great need   that the Saint grant help
When the dearest of all things   undo their union;
When the two that were married   dissolve their tie,
Their binding love,   and my soul leaves body
Going its way   I know not whither,
Not knowing the realm.   From this I shall come
To another country   according to my deeds,
And my works   that are past.   Sadly shall depart
C, Y, and **N.**   The King will be stern,
The Lord of triumph,   when stained with sin
E, W, and **U**   shall await in terror
What the Judge may ordain   according to past deeds,
As reward for life.   **L, F** shall tremble
And wretchedly wait;   shall remember the wrong,
The wounds of evil   that early or late
I wrought in the world.   In that hour weeping
I shall mourn with tears.   Too late was the time
When first I shamed me   of my deeds of sin
While body and spirit   sojourned together
United on earth.   I have need of mercy
That the Saint intercede   with the King of kings;
My need forewarns me,   and sorrow of soul.
I beseech each man   of the race of men,
Who recites this lay,   that with fervor and zeal
He will be mindful   of me by name,
And pray Heaven's Lord   to grant me help,
The God of Might   on the Great Day,
The Father and Comforter   in that fearful hour,
The Judge of deeds   and the dear Son,

* *Juliana* 695–731.

When the Trinity sitting   enthroned in glory,
One in three,   shall award to men
Through the radiant world,   according to their works,
To each man reward.   Grant us, Great God,
Thou Joy of men,   that we find Thy face
Mild with mercy   on that Great Day!   Amen.

The *Fates of the Apostles* Signature*

Now I pray the man   who may love this lay
To beseech the holy band   for help in my sorrow,
For peace and repose.   I have great need
Of gentle friends,   and kind, on the journey
When I seek out alone   my long home,
That unknown lodging,   leaving behind
This mortal body,   this bit of earth,
To serve as pillage   and plunder for worms.
   Here may a man   of clever mind,
Who has pleasure in poems,   find for himself
Who composed this poem.   *Wealth* (**F**) stands at the end;
Men have it on earth,   can not hold it forever;
Our (**U**) worldly *Joy* (**W**) fades   and the fleeting beauty
Of flesh decays   as the *Water* (**L**) flows.
Then *Brave* (**C**) and *Wretched* (**Y**)   shall seek for strength
In the weary night-watches;   upon them lies *Need* (**N**),
The service of the King.   Now can you know
Who in these words   was unknown to men.
May he remember   who loves this lay
To ask for me   God's comfort and aid.
For I must go forth   far hence alone
Seeking a home,   setting out on a journey
I know not whither   out of this world.
Unknown are those dwellings,   that region and realm.

* *Fates of the Apostles* 88–113.

Advent Lyrics *

[I]

.... to the King.

Thou art the wall-stone   the workers rejected
Of old from the work.   It befits Thee well
That Thou shouldest be Head   of the Great Hall,
Locking together   the long walls,
The flint unbroken,   in firm embrace,
That ever on earth   the eyes of all
May look with wonder   on the Lord of glory.
   With cunning skill   display Thy craft
Triumphant, Righteous,   and quickly raise
Wall against wall.   The work has need
That the Craftsman come,   the King Himself;
That He then rebuild   what now is broken,
The house under roof.   He wrought the body,
The limbs, of clay;   now the Lord of life
From their foes must rescue   this wretched host,
The woeful from dread,   as He oft has done.

[III]

   O holy Jerusalem,   Vision of peace,
Fairest of royal seats,   City of Christ,
Homeland of angels,   in thee for ever
Rest the souls   of the righteous alone
In glory exulting.   No sign of sin
In that city-dwelling   shall ever be seen;
But from thee all evil   shall flee afar,
All trouble and toil.   Thou art wondrously filled
With holy hope,   as thy name is named.

* *Christ 1* 1–17; 50–70; 249–74; 275–300.

Lift up thine eyes   on the wide Creation,
The dome of heaven,   on every hand;
Behold His coming: The King of glory
Himself approaches   to seek thee out,
To abide in thee,   as the blessed prophets
In their books foretold   the birth of the Christ,
To thy comfort spoke,   thou fairest of cities!
Now is the Babe come   born to transform
The works of the Hebrews.   He brings thee bliss,
Looses the bonds   that lie upon men;
For He it is knows   the harrowing need,
How man in his wretchedness   waits for mercy.

[VIII]

Bless earth with Thine Advent,   O Saviour Christ!
And the golden gates   which in days gone by
Full long stood locked,   High Lord of heaven,
Bid Thou swing open   and seek us out,
Humbly descending Thyself   to earth.
We have need of Thy mercy.   The dark Death-Shadow,
The Accursed Wolf,   has scattered Thy sheep
And widely dispersed them;   what Thou, O Lord,
Bought with Thy blood,   that doth the Wicked One
Take into bondage,   and smiteth sore
Against our desire.   O Saviour Lord,
In our inmost thoughts   we eagerly beg:
Hasten to help us,   miserable sinners,
That the Prince of torment   may plunge to hell;
And Thy handiwork   mount up on high,
Creator of men,   and come to righteousness,
To the beauteous realms   in the land above
From which the Dark Spirit   led us astray,
Beguiled and seduced us   through grievous sin

So that, shorn of glory,   unto all ages
We must suffer affliction,   except Thou first
O Living God,   Eternal Lord,
Shield of all creatures,   shall will to save us
Out of the clutch   of the Foe of mankind.

[IX]

  Hail, O most worthy   in all the world!
Thou purest Maiden   that ever on earth
Through the long ages   lived among men!
Rightly all mortals   in blithe mood
Name thee blessed   and hail thee Bride
Of the King of glory.   The thanes of Christ,
In heaven the highest,   carol and sing
Proclaiming thee Lady   of the heavenly legions,
Of earthly orders,   and the hosts of hell.
  Thou only of women   didst purpose of old
To bring thy maidhood   unto thy Maker,
Presenting it there   unspotted of sin.
Of all mankind   there came no other,
No bride with linked jewels,   like unto thee
With pure heart sending   thy glorious gift
To its heavenly home.   The Lord of triumph
Sent forth His herald   from the hosts on high
To bring thee knowledge   of abundant grace:
That in pure birth   thou shouldst bear God's Son
In mercy to men;   and thou thyself, Mary,
Remain for ever   Immaculate Maid.

A Dream of the Rood

Lo! I will tell   the dearest of dreams
That I dreamed in the midnight   when mortal men
Were sunk in slumber.   Me-seemed I saw
A wondrous Tree   towering in air,
Most shining of crosses   compassed with light.
Brightly that beacon   was gilded with gold;
Jewels adorned it   fair at the foot,
Five on the shoulder-beam,   blazing in splendor.
Through all creation   the angels of God
Beheld it shining—   no cross of shame!
Holy spirits   gazed on its gleaming,
Men upon earth   and all this great creation.
   Wondrous that Tree,   that Token of triumph,
And I a transgressor   soiled with my sins!
I gazed on the Rood   arrayed in glory,
Shining in beauty   and gilded with gold,
The Cross of the Saviour   beset with gems.
But through the gold-work   outgleamed a token
Of the ancient evil   of sinful men
Where the Rood on its right side   once sweat blood.
Saddened and rueful,   smitten with terror
At the wondrous Vision,   I saw the Cross
Swiftly varying   vesture and hue,
Now wet and stained   with the Blood outwelling,
Now fairly jeweled   with gold and gems.
   Then, as I lay there,   long I gazed
In rue and sadness   on my Saviour's Tree,
Till I heard in dream   how the Cross addressed me,
Of all woods worthiest,   speaking these words:
   "Long years ago   (well yet I remember)
They hewed me down   on the edge of the holt,
Severed my trunk;   strong foemen took me,

For a spectacle wrought me, a gallows for rogues.
High on their shoulders they bore me to hilltop,
Fastened me firmly, an army of foes!
   "Then I saw the King of all mankind
In brave mood hasting to mount upon me.
Refuse I dared not, nor bow nor break,
Though I felt earth's confines shudder in fear;
All foes I might fell, yet still I stood fast.
   "Then the young Warrior, God, the All-Wielder,
Put off His raiment, steadfast and strong;
With lordly mood in the sight of many
He mounted the Cross to redeem mankind.
When the Hero clasped me I trembled in terror,
But I dared not bow me nor bend to earth;
I must needs stand fast. Upraised as the Rood
I held the High King, the Lord of heaven.
I dared not bow! With black nails driven
Those sinners pierced me; the prints are clear,
The open wounds. I dared injure none.
They mocked us both. I was wet with blood
From the Hero's side when He sent forth His spirit.
   "Many a bale I bore on that hillside
Seeing the Lord in agony outstretched.
Black darkness covered with clouds God's body,
That radiant splendor. Shadow went forth
Wan under heaven; all creation wept
Bewailing the King's death. Christ was on the Cross.
   "Then many came quickly, faring from far,
Hurrying to the Prince. I beheld it all.
Sorely smitten with sorrow in meekness I bowed
To the hands of men. From His heavy and bitter pain
They lifted Almighty God. Those warriors left me
Standing bespattered with blood; I was wounded with spears.
Limb-weary they laid Him down; they stood at His head,
Looked on the Lord of heaven as He lay there at rest

From His bitter ordeal all forspent. In sight of His slayers
They made Him a sepulcher   carved from the shining stone;
Therein laid the Lord of triumph.   At evening tide
Sadly they sang their dirges   and wearily turned away
From their lordly Prince;   there He lay all still and alone.

"There at our station   a long time we stood
Sorrowfully weeping   after the wailing of men
Had died away.   The corpse grew cold,
The fair life-dwelling.   Down to earth
Men hacked and felled us,   a grievous fate!
They dug a pit   and buried us deep.
But there God's friends   and followers found me
And graced me with treasure   of silver and gold.

"Now may you learn,   O man beloved,
The bitter sorrows   that I have borne,
The work of caitiffs.   But the time is come
That men upon earth   and through all creation
Show me honor   and bow to this sign.
On me a while   God's Son once suffered;
Now I tower under heaven   in glory attired
With healing for all   that hold me in awe.
Of old I was once   the most woeful of tortures,
Most hateful to all men,   till I opened for them
The true Way of life.   Lo! the Lord of glory,
The Warden of heaven,   above all wood
Has glorified me   as Almighty God
Has honored His Mother,   even Mary herself,
Over all womankind   in the eyes of men.

"Now I give you bidding,   O man beloved,
Reveal this Vision   to the sons of men,
And clearly tell   of the Tree of glory
Whereon God suffered   for man's many sins
And the evil that Adam   once wrought of old.

"Death He suffered,   but our Saviour rose
By virtue of His great might   as a help to men.

He ascended to heaven. But hither again
He shall come unto earth   to seek mankind,
The Lord Himself   on the Day of Doom,
Almighty God   with His angel hosts.
And then will He judge,   Who has power of judgment,
To each man according   as here on earth
In this fleeting life   he shall win reward.
   "Nor there may any   be free from fear
Hearing the words   which the Wielder shall utter.
He shall ask before many: Where is the man
Who would taste bitter death   as He did on the Tree?
And all shall be fearful   and few shall know
What to say unto Christ.   But none at His Coming
Shall need to fear   if he bears in his breast
This best of symbols;   and every soul
From the ways of earth   through the Cross shall come
To heavenly glory,   who would dwell with God."
   Then with ardent spirit   and earnest zeal,
Companionless, lonely,   I prayed to the Cross.
My soul was fain of death.   I had endured
Many an hour of longing.   It is my life's hope
That I may turn   to this Token of triumph,
I above all men,   and revere it well.
   This is my heart's desire,   and all my hope
Waits on the Cross.   In this world now
I have few powerful friends;   they have fared hence
Away from these earthly gauds   seeking the King of glory,
Dwelling now with the High Father   in heaven above,
Abiding in rapture.   Each day I dream
Of the hour when the Cross of my Lord,   whereof here on earth
I once had vision,   from this fleeting life may fetch me
And bring me where is great gladness   and heavenly bliss,
Where the people of God   are planted and stablished for ever
In joy everlasting.   There may it lodge me
Where I may abide in glory   knowing bliss with the saints.

May the Lord be gracious   who on earth of old
Once suffered on the Cross   for the sins of men.
He redeemed us, endowed us with life   and a heavenly home.
Therein was hope renewed   with blessing and bliss
For those who endured the burning.   In that great deed
God's Son was triumphant,   possessing power and strength!
Almighty, Sole-Ruling   He came to the kingdom of God
Bringing a host of souls   to angelic bliss,
To join the saints   who abode in the splendor of glory,
When the Lord, Almighty God,   came again to His throne.

The Last Judgment *

Suddenly in the midnight   on mortal men
The Great Day of the Lord God   shall come with might,
Filling with fear   the fair Creation,
Like a wily thief   who walks in darkness,
A robber bold   in the black night
Who suddenly assails   men fast in slumber,
Lying in wait for the unwary   and the unprepared.
   So on Mount Sion   a mighty host
Shall gather together   faithful to God,
Bright and blithe;   they shall know bliss.
From the four regions   of earth's realm,
From the uttermost corners   of earth's kingdom,
All-shining angels   in unison sounding
Shall blow their trumpets   in a great blast.
The earth shall tremble,   the mold under men.
Loud shall resound   the strains of the trumpets
Swelling clear   to the course of the stars.
They shall peal and sing   from south and north,
From east and west   over all creation.
They shall wake from death   the sons of warriors,
All mankind,   from the ancient earth
To the terror of Judgment,   telling them rise,
Start up straightway   from their deep sleep. . . .
   Suddenly on Mount Sion   from the south and east
Shall come from the Creator   light like the sun
Shining more bright   than men may imagine,
Gleaming in splendor,   when the Son of God
Through the arching heavens   hither appears.
Then comes the wondrous   presence of Christ,
The glory of the Great King,   from the eastern skies,
Cordial and kind   to His own people,
Severe to the sinful,   wondrously varying:

* *Christ 3* 867–89; 899–991; 1027–38; 1061–1102; 1634–64.

Unto the blessed   and the forlorn unlike!
   To all the good   He is gracious of aspect,
Winsome and blithe   to that holy band,
Joyous and loving,   a gentle Friend.
'Tis a pleasant sight   and sweet to His dear ones,
That shining beauty   gentle in joy,
The Coming of the Saviour,   the King of might,
To all who earlier   here on earth
Pleased Him well   by their words and works.
   But to transgressors,   to guilty souls
Who come before Him   destroyed by sin
He shall be fearful   and frightful to see.
This may serve as a warning   of woe for sinners
That a man of wisdom   need feel no dismay,
No whit of dread   in the Day of Doom.
In the face of that terror   he shall not fear
When he sees the Shaper   of all Creation
Moving to Judgment   with wondrous might,
And round Him circling   on every side
The angel multitude   in shining muster,
Hosts of the holy   throng upon throng.
   There is din through the deep Creation.   Before God
The greatest of raging fires   flames over earth.
The hot blaze surges,   the heavens shall fall;
The steadfast light   of the stars shall fail.
The sun shall be blackened   to the hue of blood
Which shone so brightly   for the sons of men
Over the ancient earth.   The moon herself
That by night illumined   mankind with her light
Shall sink from her station;   so also the stars
Swept by the whirlwind   through the storm-beat air
Shall vanish from heaven.
                              With His angel host
The Lord of kings   shall come to the Judgment,
The glorious Ruler;   His gladsome thanes,
The hosts of the holy,   shall attend their Lord
When the Prince of men   amid pangs of terror

Himself shall seek out   the peoples of earth.
    Then loud shall be heard   through the wide world
The sound of heaven's trumpet;   on seven sides
The winds shall rage   raving in uproar;
They shall wake and wither   the world with storm;
They shall fill with fear   the creatures of earth.
Then shall be heard   the heaviest of crashes,
Mighty and deafening,   a measureless blast,
The greatest of tumults,   terrible to men.
    There the doomed hordes   and hosts of mankind
Shall turn away   to the towering flames
Where consuming fire   shall seize them alive,
Some above, some below,   filled full of flame.
Then shall be clear   how the kin of Adam
Full of sorrow   weep in distress,
Nor for little cause,   those hapless legions,
But for the greatest   of all griefs
When the dark surge of fire,   the dusky flame,
Seizes all three: the seas with their fish,
The earth with her hills,   and the high heavens
Bright with stars.   The destroying fire
In fiercest fury   shall burn all three
Grimly together.   And all the earth
Shall moan in misery   in that awful hour.
    So the greedy spirit,   the despoiling brands,
Shall search through earth   and her high-built halls;
The wide-known blaze   burning and greedy
Shall fill the world   with a terror of flame.
Broken city-walls   shall crumble and crash;
Mountains shall melt,   and the high cliffs
Which in olden days   shielded the earth
Stout and steadfast   against the floods,
Barriers against the waters,   the breaking waves.
    In that dread hour   the death-fire shall clutch
Every creature   of bird and beast.
The fire-dark flame   shall fare through earth
A raging warrior.   As waters of old,

The rushing floods, flowed over earth,
In that hour shall burn   in a bath of fire
All the fishes   cut off from the sea;
All beasts of the deep   shall wretchedly die.
Water shall burn like wax.   And then shall be
More of marvels   than man can imagine:
How the thunder and storm   and the wild wind
Shatter the wide Creation. . . .
   Straightway all   of Adam's kin
Shall be clothed with flesh,   shall come to an end
Of their rest in earth;   each of mankind
Shall rise up living,   put on body and limbs,
Made young again   at the Coming of Christ.
Each shall have on him   of evil or good
All his soul garnered   in years gone by,
Shall have both together,   body and soul.
Then the manner of his works,   and the memory of his words,
The hidden musing   of his inmost heart,
Shall come to light   before heaven's King. . . .
   Then the trumpet's strain   and the shining standard,
The fiery heat   and the heavenly host,
The throng of angels   and the throes of fear,
The Day of terror   and the towering Cross
Upraised as a sign   of the Ruler's might,
Shall summon mankind   before the King,
Every soul   that early or late
Was fashioned in flesh   with limbs and body.
   Then the greatest of legions,   living and young,
Shall go before the face   of the Lord God.
By need and by desire   known by their names
They shall bring to God's Son   the hoard of the breast,
The jewels of life.   The Father will learn
How safely his sons   have guarded their souls
In the former land   where they lived on earth.
   Those shall be bold   who bring unto God
A shining beauty.   Their strength and joy
Shall be greatly abundant   to bless their souls,

To reward their works. Well is it with them
Who find favor with God   in that grim hour!
    There sin-stained men   in anguish of spirit
Shall see as their fate   the most fearful of woes:
It shall bring them no grace   that the brightest of beacons,
The Rood of our Saviour,   red with His blood,
Over-run with bright gore,   upreared before men,
With radiant light   shall illumine the wide Creation.
No shadows shall lurk   where the light of the Cross
Streams on all nations.   Yet shall it stand
As a woe and a menace   for evil men,
Sinners who gave   no thanks to God
That for man's transgressions   He grievously hung
On the holy Tree,   where with love our Lord
Bought life for men   with His ransoming body
(Which had wrought no evil   nor any wrong)
Whereby He redeemed us.   For that He ordains
A stern requital   when the red-stained Rood
Shall shine in splendor   in the place of the sun. . . .
    Then chosen souls   shall bring before Christ
Their bright treasures;   their bliss shall live
In the Day of Doom.   They shall joy with God
In the sweet life   assigned to the saints
In the heavenly kingdom.   That is the home
That knows no ending,   but there for ever
The pure have delight   in praising the Lord,
Dear Warden of life,   in light encompassed,
Swathed in peace,   shielded from sorrow,
Honored with grace,   endeared unto God.
Always for ever   the angel band
Bright with glory   shall blissfully joy
In the worship of God.   The Warden of all
Shall have and shall hold   the hosts of the holy.
    There is song of angels   and bliss of the saints,
The Saviour's dear presence   shining more bright
On all His beloved   than light of the sun.
There is love of dear ones;   life without death;

Exultant multitudes;   youth without age;
The splendor of heaven's hosts;   health without pain;
For the souls of the righteous   rest without toil.
There is glory of the saints;   day without darkness
Bright with blessing;   bliss without sorrow;
Accord among friends   without envy for ever
For the happy in heaven;   love without hate
In that holy throng.   No hunger there nor thirst,
Nor sleep nor sickness   nor burning sun,
Nor cold nor care.   But the band of the blessed,
Most shining of legions,   shall delight for ever
In the grace of the King   and glory with God.

IX

HISTORIC BATTLE POEMS

HISTORIC BATTLE POEMS

An entry in the *Anglo-Saxon Chronicle* for the year 793 records the first of the Danish raids on the Northumbrian coast. By 866 the raiding expeditions had been followed by permanent encampment on English soil. In 870 the *Chronicle* records the havoc wrought at Medhamsted to which the Danes came, "burning and breaking and slaying Abbot and monks and all that they found." It is fitting that the defense of England in the ninth and tenth centuries should be symbolized in Old English poetry by the memorable poems of *Brunanburh* and *Maldon*.

The Battle of Brunanburh is one of a group of short poems included among the entries in the *Chronicle*, in this instance for the year 937. In it patriotic spirit and a note of national destiny receive dramatic expression. The poem has sometimes been misunderstood because of its failure to name individual heroes, or recount individual exploits. But *Brunanburh* was never intended to be a detailed description of the battle. It is rather a chant of triumph celebrating one of those decisive military successes that mark the development of national unity and national strength. The precise location of the battle has not been identified with certainty, but Bosworth placed the battle "about five miles southwest of Durham."

The Battle of Maldon was preserved in a manuscript of the Cotton collection. It celebrates a bitter but glorious defeat, whereas *Brunanburh* celebrates a great victory. According to the account of the battle in an entry in the *Chronicle* for 991, the Viking forces sailed up the Blackwater (Panta) and established a temporary base near Maldon. Laborde (*English Historical Review* xi, 161) believes that this base was on Northey Island, from which the invaders crossed to the mainland at the beginning of the battle. From the western end of the island the river bed ridges up into a ford to the mainland, which is partly exposed at low tide, but completely covered at high water. This is presumably the "bricg" or "ford" of lines 74, 78, 81, and 88 of the poem.

The death of Byrhtnoth, leader of the English forces, is followed in the poem by the most extended and realistic depiction of *comitatus* loyalty in Old English verse. The poet calls the bloody roll of honor. Warrior after warrior is named, and his heroism recounted. Fighting shoulder to shoulder with the young and strong, the aged Byrhtwold glorified his last battle with a clarion call to fortitude and death, whose echo lives while friendship and loyalty are dear and men defend the things they love. His words set the mood of all heroic striving in which deep-seated devotion to a moral imperative breeds a contempt for the odds of battle.

The Battle of Brunanburh

Æthelstan King,   lord of eorls,
Ring-bestower,   and also his brother,
Edmund Ætheling,   won with the sword-edge
Lifelong glory   in battle at Brunanburh.
They cut their way   through the wall of shields,
Hacked the bucklers   with hammered blades.
Such was the way   of the sons of Eadweard,
Ever in battle   with every foe
Defending their land,   their hoard and their homes.
Foemen fell,   the Scottish squadrons,
Ship-warriors also   doomed to death.
The field was wet   with the blood of battle
From the hour of dawn   when the shining sun,
God's radiant candle,   rose over earth
Till the noble creation   sank to its setting.
Wounded with spears   lay many a warrior,
Many a northern man   shot over shield;
Scotsmen likewise   sated with war.
  All day long   the West Saxon army
Followed the track   of the hated foe,
Smote them down   with sharp-edged swords.
The Mercians refused   fierce hand-play to none
Of those who with Olaf   over the sea
Sought this land   in their broad-beamed ships,
Fated in war.   Five young kings
Fell on the battlefield   slain with swords;
Also seven   of the eorls of Olaf
And a countless number   of shipmen and Scots.
The prince of the Northmen   was put to flight,
With a little band   beaten back to his boat.
The ship was launched;   the prince set sail
On the fallow surges   and saved his skin.
  Likewise also   the aged Constantine

Fled in haste   to his home in the north;
The white-haired warrior   had no need to boast
Of that crossing of swords.   He was shorn of kin,
Bereft of friends   struck down in the fight
On the field of carnage.   There amid corpses
He left his son,   a stripling in battle
Broken with wounds.   The gray-haired warrior,
The crafty old captain,   had no cause to boast
Of the clash of swords,   nor had Olaf any!
The few that were left   had no need to laugh,
Or boast they were better   in works of war,
On the field of battle,   mid clash of banners,
Crashing of fighters   and casting of spears,
In the storm of weapons,   the carnage of war,
When they fought their fight   with the sons of Eadweard.
　　The Northmen embarked   in their well-nailed boats,
Bloody survivors   of battle-spears,
Over Dinges Water   returning to Dublin,
Back to Ireland,   broken in mood.
Likewise also   the brothers together,
King and prince   returned to their people,
To the West Saxon country,   proud of the war.
They left behind them   to feast on the fallen
The dark raven,   the dusky-coated
With horny beak,   and the ash-feathered eagle
With white tail,   and the war-hawk greedy
Gorging on carrion,   and that gray beast,
The wolf in the wood.   Nor of greater slaughter
In all this island   was tale ever told
By scholar or book,   or more folk felled
Slain by the sword,   since hither from East
The Angles and Saxons   sailed over sea,
Over broad billows   seeking out Britain,
Great-hearted war-smiths   eager for honor
Who harried the Welshmen   and held the land.

The Battle of Maldon

        .... was broken.
He bade a warrior   abandon his horse
And hurry forward   to join the fighters,
Take thought to his hands   and a stout heart.
Then Offa's kinsmen   knew that the eorl
Would never suffer   weakness or fear;
And he let from hand   his beloved hawk
Fly to the forest,   and made haste to the front;
By which one could know   the lad would never
Weaken in war   when he seized a sword.
   Eadric also   stood by his lord,
His prince, in the battle;   forward he bore
His spear to the fight;   he had firm resolve
While he could hold   in hard hand-grip
Broad sword and buckler;   he made good his boast
That he would battle   beside his lord.
   Byrhtnoth began   to hearten his fighters;
He rode and gave counsel,   instructing the men
How they should stand   and defend the spot.
He bade that they hold   their bucklers aright
Firm in their hands,   and be not afraid.
When he had fairly   mustered the folk
He lighted down   where it liked him well,
Where he knew his retainers   were truest and best.
   Then stood on the strand   and boldly shouted
The Viking herald,   boastfully hurled
To the eorl on the shore   the shipmen's message:
"These dauntless seamen   have sent me to you,
Bade me say   you must quickly send
Riches for ransom;   better for you
That you buy off with tribute   a battle of spears
Than that we should wage   hard war against you.
Nor need we waste strength   if you will consent;

But we for the gold   will confirm a peace.
If you will agree,   who are greatest here,
To ransom your people   and promise to pay
On their own terms   unto the shipmen
Gold for goodwill,   and have peace at our hands,
We with the treasure   will take to our ships,
Put to sea,   and observe the peace."
    Byrhtnoth addressed him;   brandished his shield;
Shook pliant ash-spear;   speaking with words
Enraged and resolute,   gave him answer:
"Hear you, sea-rover,   what my people say?
The tribute they'll send you   is tribute of spears,
Ancient sword-edge   and poisoned point,
Weapons availing you   little in war!
Pirate messenger,   publish this answer,
Proclaim to your people   tidings more grim:
Here stands no ignoble   eorl with his army
Guarding my lord Æthelred's   country and coast,
His land and his folk.   The heathen shall fall
In the clash of battle.   Too shameful it seems
That you with our tribute   should take to your ships
Unfought, when thus far   you've invaded our land.
You shall not so easily   take our treasure,
But sword-edge and spear-point   first shall decide,
The grim play of battle,   ere tribute is granted."
    Then he bade bear buckler,   warriors advance
And form their ranks   on the river's edge;
Not yet, for the tide,   could either attack.
The flood-tide was flowing   after the ebb,
And the currents locked.   Too long it seemed
Till men to battle   might bear their spears.
Near Panta River   in proud array
Stood the East Saxon host   and the Viking horde;
Nor could either army   do harm to the other
Except who through arrow-flight   found his death.
    Then the flood-tide ebbed;   the raiders stood ready,
The pirate army   eager for war.

The lord commanded   a war-hardened man
To defend the ford,   Wulfstan his name,
Brave among kinsmen,   Ceola's son.
He wounded with weapon   the foremost man
Who first there fiercely   set foot on the ford.
At Wulfstan's shoulder   stood fearless fighters,
Ælfere and Maccus,   a mighty pair.
Never would such   take flight at the ford!
But they bravely defended   against the foe
What time they were able   to wield their weapons.
   When the pirates perceived   and clearly saw
That they had been met   by bitter bridge-wardens,
The Viking shipmen   began to dissemble,
Asked for permission   to make approach,
To fare over ford   and take their troops.
It was then the eorl   disdainfully granted
Too much ground   to the hostile host.
Across cold water   Byrhthelm's son
Shouted reply,   and the shipmen hearkened:
"Now way is made open,   come quickly to us,
Warriors to the onset;   God only knows
Who shall hold sway   on the field of slaughter."
   The war-wolves advanced,   heeded not water,
West across Panta;   the Viking host
Over shining water   carried their shields.
Among his warriors   Byrhtnoth stood bold
Against the grim foe;   bade form with shields
The war-hedge for battle,   hold firm the folk
Against the foemen.   Then fighting was near,
Honor in battle.   The hour was come
Doomed men must fall.   A din arose.
Raven and eagle   were eager for carnage;
There was uproar on earth.   Men let from their hands
File-hard darts   and sharp spears fly.
Bows were busy,   shield stopped point,
Bitter was the battle-rush.   Warriors fell
In both the armies.   Young men lay dead.

Wulfmær was wounded;   Byrhtnoth's kin,
His sister's son,   was savagely butchered
Choosing the slaughter-bed,   slain with the sword.
    Then to the seamen   requital was made.
I have heard that Eadweard   slew one with sword,
Withheld not the blow;   the fated fighter
Fell at his feet.   And for that the prince
Thanked his retainer   when later was time.
So resisted   the stout of heart,
Young men in battle;   boldly strove
Who first with spear,   warrior with weapon,
Could visit death   on life that was doomed.
There was slaughter on earth;   steadfast they stood,
And Byrhtnoth heartened them,   bidding each man
Take thought to the war   who would win from the Danes.
    The battle-hard brandished   his weapon for war,
His shield for defense,   and stormed at the foe;
Even so bold   went eorl against churl.
Both purposed evil,   each for the other.
Then the shipman cast   a southern spear
And the lord of warriors   suffered a wound.
He thrust with his shield   so the shaft was shattered,
The lance was broken,   the parts fell back.
The prince was angered;   he stung with his spear
The arrogant Viking   who gave him the wound.
He fought with skill   driving his dart
Through the pirate's throat;   he thrust with hand
So he touched the life   of the savage foe.
Then most quickly   he cast another
And the byrny burst.   He was wounded in breast
Through his woven mail,   and the poisoned point
Bit at his heart.   The eorl was the blither;
The proud man laughed,   gave thanks to God
For that day's work   which the Lord had granted.
    But one of the shipmen   hurled from his hand
A flying spear;   and the speeding dart
Pierced through Æthelred's   princely thane.

A stripling lad   stood at his shoulder,
A boy in the battle,   who bravely drew
The bloody spear   from the warrior's side,
Wulmær the youthful,   Wulfstan's son.
Back he hurled   the battle-hard dart;
The point pierced in   and he sank to earth
Whose hand had given   the grievous hurt.
   Then a pirate warrior   went to the eorl;
Soon would he seize   his jewels and gems,
His armor of rings,   and his well-wrought sword.
But Byrhtnoth snatched   his sword from the sheath,
Broad and brown-edged,   and struck at his byrny.
Too speedily one   of the shipmen hindered,
Striking aside   the arm of the eorl;
And the gold-hilted sword   fell to the ground,
Nor might he hold longer   the hard blade,
Or wield his weapon.   Once more he spoke;
The aged ruler   rallied his men,
Bade them go forward   and bear them well.
No more could he stand   firm on his feet,
But he looked to heaven. . . .
   "I give Thee thanks,   O God of men,
For all the joys   I have had on earth.
O Lord of mercy,   I have most need
That now Thou wilt grant me   good to my soul,
That my spirit may come   into Thy kingdom,
O Prince of angels,   departing in peace
Into Thy power.   To Thee I pray
No fiend of hell   may have hold upon me."
Then the heathen scoundrels   hacked him down
And both the fighters   who stood at his side.
Ælfnoth and Wulmær   both were fallen;
They laid down their lives   beside their lord.
   Then fled from the battle   who feared to be there:
The sons of Odda   were first in flight,
Godric from battle,   leaving his lord
Who had given him many   a goodly steed;

He leaped on the horse   that belonged to his leader,
Rode in the trappings   that were not his right,
And his brothers with him   both galloped off.
Godrinc and Godwig   recked not of war,
But turned from the fighting,   took to the wood,
Fled to the fastness,   and saved their lives;
And more of men   than was any way right
If they had remembered   the many gifts
Their lord had given them   to their good.
As Offa once said,   at an earlier time
In the meeting-place   when he held assembly,
That many were there   making brave boasts
Who would never hold out   in the hour of need.
Then was fallen   the lord of the folk,
Æthelred's eorl;   and his hearth-companions
All beheld   that their lord lay dead.
  Forward they pressed,   the proud retainers,
Fiercely charged   those fearless thanes.
Each of them wished   one thing of two:
To avenge his leader   or lose his life.
Ælfric's son   spurred them to battle,
A warrior young;   in words that were bold
Ælfwine spoke,   undaunted of spirit:
  "Take thought of the times   when we talked at mead,
Seated on benches   making our boasts,
Warriors in hall,   concerning hard battle.
Now comes the test   who truly is bold!
I purpose to prove   my lineage to all men:
That in Mercia I come   of a mighty clan;
Ealhelm the name   of my aged father,
A powerful ealdorman   wealthy and wise.
None shall reproach me   among that people
That I was willing   to slink from the strife,
Hastening home   when my lord lies dead,
Slain in the battle.   Of all disasters
That to me   is the greatest of griefs,
For he was my kinsman;   he was my lord."

Then he dashed forward,   took thought of the feud;
One of the shipmen   he stabbed with spear
Among the folk,   and he fell to earth
Slain with weapon.   He encouraged his comrades,
Friends and companions   to press to the front.
   Offa spoke   and brandished his ash-spear:
"Now hast thou, Ælfwine,   heartened us all
In the hour of need.   Now our lord lies dead,
Our eorl on earth,   there is need that we all,
Each of us here   embolden the others,
Warriors to combat,   while hand may bear
Good sword and spear,   and hold hard blade.
This sneaking Godric,   Odda's son,
Has betrayed us all;   for when he rode off
Sitting on horse,   on our lord's proud steed,
Many men weened   that it was our lord.
On the field of fate now   the folk is divided,
The shield-hedge is shattered;   cursed be his deed
That he caused so many   to flee from the fight."
   Leofsunu spoke,   lifted his buckler,
His board for protection,   making his boast:
"I promise you here   I will never turn hence
Or flee one foot,   but I'll fight in the front,
In the bitter strife,   and avenge my lord.
Steadfast warriors   by the River Stour
Shall never have need   of words to reproach me,
Now my lord is fallen,   that lordless I fled,
Turned back from the battle   and went to my home;
But weapon shall take me,   sword-edge and spear."
Then in rage   he rushed to the fighting
Despising to flee.   Dunnere shook spear,
The aged churl,   called out to them all,
Bidding take vengeance   for Byrhtnoth's fall:
"He may not weaken   who thinks to avenge
His lord on this folk,   nor fear for his life."
Then they rushed forward,   recked not of life,

Household-retainers   fierce in the fight,
Bitter spear-bearers   beseeching God
They might work revenge   for their friendly lord
In death and destruction   upon the foe.
   Then a hostage began   to give them help,
Of Northumbrian race   and hardy kin,
A son of Ecglaf,   Æscferth his name.
He wavered not   in the midst of the war-play
But forward pressed   to the arrow-flight,
Now shooting on shield,   now piercing a shipman,
But oft and often   dealing a wound,
While he could wield   his weapon in war.
   In front line still   stood Eadweard the long,
Skillful and eager;   he spoke his boast:
That he would not flee   foot-measure of ground
Nor turn from the battle   where his better lay dead.
He shattered the shield-wall   and fought with the Danes.
Upon the shipmen   he stoutly avenged
His gracious lord   ere he sank in the slaughter.
So did Ætheric,   excellent comrade,
Sibyrht's brother;   he boldly strove
Eager and ready;   and many another
Stood their ground   and shattered the shields.
Bucklers broke,   and byrnies sang
A song of terror.   Then Offa smote
One of the shipmen   and laid him low;
But Gadd's kinsman also   fell in the fight.
Quickly in battle   was Offa cut down.
But he had performed   what he promised his lord,
When he made his boast   to his bracelet-bestower,
That both unharmed   they would ride to the borough,
Back to their homes,   or fall in the fight
And perish of wounds   in the place of slaughter.
Thane-like he lay   beside his lord.
   Then was breaking of bucklers,   shipmen advanced
Bold to the battle;   sharp spears pierced
Life-house of doomed men.   Wistan hastened,

Thurstan's son,   and strove with the Danes.
Three he slew   in the stress of battle
Ere Wiglin's son   was slain in the war.
The strife was stern,   warriors were steadfast,
Bold in battle;   fighters fell
Weary with wounds.   Death covered earth.
Oswold and Ealdwald   all the while,
Both the brothers,   marshalled their men;
Bade friend and kinsman   endure in combat
And never weaken,   but wield the sword.
    Byrhtwold encouraged them,   brandishing buckler,
Aged companion   shaking ash-spear;
Stout were the words   he spoke to his men:
    "Heart must be braver,   courage the bolder,
Mood the stouter   as our strength grows less!
Here on the ground   my good lord lies
Gory with wounds.   Always will he regret it
Who now from this battle   thinks to turn back.
I am old in years;   I will never yield,
But here at the last   beside my lord,
By the leader I love   I think to lie."
    And Godric to battle   heartened them all;
Æthelgar's son   hurled many a spear
At the Viking horde.   First in the front
He hacked and hewed   till he fell in the slaughter.
He was not the Godric   who fled from the fight. . . .

INDEX

INDEX OF SELECTIONS